Harley-Davidson
1903–1968

JOHN CARROLL

SUTTON PUBLISHING

Sutton Publishing Limited
Phoenix Mill · Thrupp · Stroud
Gloucestershire · GL5 2BU

First published 2001

Title page: A WLA, see pages 70–1.

British Library Cataloguing in Publication Data
A catalogue record for this book is available from the
British Library.

ISBN 0-7509-2342-3

Typeset in 10.5/13.5 Photina.
Typesetting and origination by
Sutton Publishing Limited.
Printed and bound in England by
J.H. Haynes & Co. Ltd, Sparkford.

Dr Ian 'Maz' Harris. Hell's Angels MC, Kent, England, 26.7.49–31.5.00. Maz, it was a privilege to have known you.

'Harley-Davidson: Motorcycling's Pacesetter for 1941'. An advert from *The Enthusiast* with no hint at the events that were unfolding on the world stage. The 1941 range motorcycles were the last civilian Harleys offered before the end of the Second World War because the Japanese air strike against Pearl Harbor in December that year brought the US into the conflict that had been raging in Europe since 1939. (GS)

Contents

A Canadian Army Sergeant riding a 1942 WLC Harley-Davidson through Lindford Ford, Hampshire, on 14 October 1942. He is being closely followed by another rider on a Norton 16H. The third rider in the water, also on a WLC, is Captain Jerry Bradshaw, a Canadian Training School (CTS) instructor. The training of Canadian despatch riders (DR) was reputed to be tough. (NMM)

Preface

Switch the petrol tap on, select neutral with the hand gearstick, engage the clutch with the foot-operated lever, a touch of choke, twist the throttle twice, switch the ignition on and kick down on the bicycle-type starter pedal. With a compression ratio of only 4.75:1 the old motorcycle rarely fails to go first kick. By the time I've pulled my helmet and gloves on the engine has settled down into the uneven but rhythmic beat that characterises a 45 degree V-twin. This particular one, a Harley-Davidson, was made in 1942 and displaces only 45 cubic inches. Riding it is the realisation of a long-cherished dream. For me that dream combines a fascination with social history, military vehicles, old motorcycles in general and Harley-Davidsons in particular. This Harley-Davidson is one of approximately 88,000 made for the Allies in the Second World War, a WLC. Its designation means it is a military WL produced for the Canadian Army to a standard specification that varied slightly from the American Army's WLA (the C suffix indicates Canada: the A suffix indicates Army). Suffixes and specifications may be as dry as a Latin lesson on a summer afternoon but this is my bike. It is more than simply one of 88,000. It is a tangible link with one of the most turbulent periods of the twentieth century.

I often wonder who rode this bike in those troubled days; did some grim-faced Canadian despatcher escort the ambulances away from the docks on it after survivors struggled back into English ports following the débâcle at Dieppe? Did some young man from Winnipeg name it after the girlfriend he had left thousands of miles away? Or did someone ride it while day-dreaming of a canoe and the cool clear waters of the Algonquin? I will never know but that doesn't stop me wondering.

Those of us fascinated with the minutiae of Second World War military Harleys are familiar with the photograph (reproduced here) of a Canadian sergeant riding a WLC through a ford 'somewhere in England' on a training exercise. The first time I saw the 45 that was to become mine I was immediately reminded of the photograph. The bike's then owner arrived at a vintage rally one Sunday morning on the original-looking machine. Restored but not overdone, it had almost all the requisite genuine parts, including the additional toolbox on top of the front mudguard that instantly identifies it as a Canadian-specification machine. Both front and rear stands were fitted, as were Canadian-pattern lights. Wedged under the seat was a 'for sale' sign. I just had to have that bike. Monday morning found me arranging some finance. The words 'Harley-Davidson' did the trick and the finance company, no doubt assuming I was considerably better heeled than I really was, sent me away with a cheque.

Once the bike was unloaded from the hire van I learned to ride it on the lane that runs away from my house. The hand-shift and foot-clutch arrangement is easier than it looks because the foot pedal for the clutch can be left in the disengaged position, allowing the left foot to be put down on the road at junctions. The low seat helps too and before long I was piloting the machine along the back lanes between drystone walls, pogoing gently on the sprung saddle. The acid test of my ability was

The author's 1942 Canadian Army WLC 'somewhere in England' but more than fifty years after the CTS rode bikes like this through Lindford Ford in Hampshire. (JC)

Huddersfield's small but busy ring road; hand signals, hand gearshifts, the ignition advance and retard left twistgrip, and rubber-necking motorists all had to be coped with. I really wasn't prepared for the level of interest generated by an old, green Harley.

The vintage flathead elicits a variety of reactions. Some can't believe it can be ridden while others look at it more nostalgically. At a rally an elderly chap recounted to me how he'd bought one war surplus in the late '40s. His friend had acquired a 741 Indian and apparently great rivalry soon developed between them. I couldn't help but smile as I imagined the two friends roaring around Oxfordshire lanes, unknowingly acting out the old factory rivalry between the two companies. Through the '30s and '40s it was the Harley v Indian competition that made motorcycle racing on dirt tracks the length and breadth of America the spectacle it most certainly was. The bikes weren't that far removed from their khaki cousins: the 45 cubic inch Harley-Davidson WLDR and Indian Sport Scout were the bikes on which Bert 'Campy' Campanale and 'Ironman' Ed Kretz slid sideways into the sand turns at Daytona as Europe slid inexorably towards war.

Later I bought a Harley Evolution Sportster. It's convenient; you just switch it on and ride away. It's also nimble, reliable and fun but it doesn't have the clatter and 'vintageness' of the flathead. Over the years other bikes have come and gone from my possession, Triumphs and similar, even a Kawasaki-engined chopper, but the WLC is here to stay.

Normandy in 1994, remembering 1944; proud old men with medal ribbons on their jackets wandered among the restored military vehicles that had once been so familiar to them. Their eyes fixed on one that brought back memories and, hands trembling, they touched the matt green paint and began, 'Do you know son . . .'. Harley-Davidson, the freedom machine indeed.

Introduction

The surnames of two families, Harley and Davidson, both European immigrants to the United States, combined to form one of the most recognised brands of motorcycle in the world. Harley-Davidson stands for more than just a motorcycle, though. It is now an American icon, the embodiment of America on two wheels. The attentions of Hollywood's film-makers have no doubt helped the Harley-Davidson achieve its current status – *Easy Rider*, *Electraglide in Blue*, *Mask* and *The Loveless* are prominent among a host of motorcycle movies.

The first boom in motorcycle manufacture occurred in the very early years of the twentieth century as the mode of transport changed image from complex novelty to practical proposition. The development of the automobile was progressing in parallel, and some of the earliest motorcyclists were those who added internal-combustion engines to bicycles. Many of the earliest manufacturers of motorcycles were established bicycle makers who saw the internal-combustion engine as simply another bicycle component. The Federation of American Motorcyclists (FAM) was founded in late 1903. It went on to become the American Motorcyclist Association (AMA) and the sport of motorcycling's governing body.

The only surviving American motorcycle manufacturer – Harley-Davidson – was founded in 1903, although the number of bikes the company made in that first year can be counted on the fingers of a single hand. Harley-Davidson wasn't the first either: the Hendee and Hedstrom concern, manufacturers of Indian motorcycles, had been formed in 1901 on the strength of the pair's diverse but overlapping interests in the world of competitive bicycling.

From the earliest days there was competition to offer the most reliable, fastest, best or cheapest machine, and this rivalry intensified as the number of manufacturers rose (reaching a peak of 250). It spilled over into racetrack-type events as manufacturers realised that the spectacle of speed drew crowds eager to see the thrills and spills – and possibly become motorcyclists, and therefore customers, themselves. Lubrication systems, starting mechanisms, ignition systems and controls were quickly refined. Gradually the accepted formula for motorcycles became hand throttle, foot clutch, hand gearshift. Final drive was either by leather belt or chain; both were perceived as having advantages and disadvantages, although the advent of a functional clutch mechanism ultimately led to chain final drive being favoured for approximately eighty years. Controls were variously mounted on the handlebars and in brackets on the sides of the gas tanks. Two engine configurations soon became dominant – singles and V-twins – although the US motorcycle industry persevered with in-line air-cooled four-cylinder machines right up to the outbreak of the Second World War. As early as 1906 spring forks, purpose-designed frames and magneto ignition were in use, albeit far from universal. The motorcycle was beginning to catch on. Companies adopted adventurous and exciting names for themselves and their products – Flying Merkel, Peerless, Cyclone –

Harley-Davidson range brochures from 1923, 1925 and 1928. (GS)

and advertising copy writers glorified the new form of transport. Iver Johnson described its motorcycles as 'Exquisite Mechanisms'; 'Hit the Indian trail . . . to health and high adventure', said Indian; and 'No limit to speed but the law', boasted Reading Standard. 'This motorcycle does the work of three horses', claimed Harley-Davidson.

There is a huge amount of jargon associated with Harley-Davidsons, so to provide an insight for those new to the marque a few pointers follow. 'Flatheads' were built between 1929 and 1973 in various capacities including 45, 55, 74 and 80 cubic inch displacements. 'Knuckleheads', overhead-valve machines, were built from 1936 to 1947 in 61 and 74 cubic inch displacements. 'Panheads' were updated overhead-valve machines built between 1948 and 1965 in 61 and 74 cubic inch sizes. 'Generator Shovelheads' were built in 74 cubic inch displacement only between 1966 and 1969. 'Alternator Shovelheads' were manufactured from 1970 to 1983 in 74 cubic inch displacements. 'Sportsters' have been made from 1957 to date in 55, 61 and 74 cubic inch displacements. Throughout its history the company has also experimented with a number of smaller capacity motorcycles, including the Hummer, a 125cc German DKW-inspired machine, in the postwar years and the Italian Aermacchi lightweights in the '60s. However, the story of the Harley-Davidson is much more than capacities and model designations, as the nicknames above might indicate.

Using a selection of archive photographs from a number of sources, this book considers the history of Harley-Davidson from its humble beginnings in a Wisconsin shed in 1903 up to 1968 when acquisition by the industrial conglomerate American Machine and Foundry (AMF) was just around the corner. AMF's ownership lasted for sixteen years and by 1984 the company was again independent. The early '70s were boom years for motorcycle sales and AMF-controlled Harley-Davidson upped production enormously. This move compounded quality control problems. Although AMF is frequently criticised for its ownership of Harley-Davidson and the way it ran the operation, it is generally accepted that if AMF had not bought the company, Harley would not have survived. Survive it did, however, and since 1984 there have been two new Big Twin engines – the Evolution and the Twin Cam – and the company is again enjoying booming sales of its products.

Chronology

1903	First Harley-Davidson made
1913	Export sales of Harley-Davidsons begin
1916	Harley-Davidson's magazine *The Enthusiast* first published
1917	US enters the First World War on the side of the Allies
1929	**October** Wall Street Crash
1932	First Harley-Davidson Servicar models built
1936	Model 61E ohv Knucklehead introduced
1937	Harley-Davidson Model U launched as upgraded Model V
1939	**3 September** Second World War starts in Europe
1940	**June** British Army evacuated from France as it falls to Germany
1941	**7 December** Japanese air attack on Pearl Harbor
1945	**8 May** Victory in Europe (VE) Day
1945	**14 August** Japan surrenders
1947	Resumption of racing at Daytona, Florida
1948	**March** First chapter of Hell's Angels Motorcycle Club formed in California
1948	61cid EL and 74cid FL Panheads introduced
1949	Hydra-Glide hydraulic front forks introduced
1953	**2 December** Indian announces end of its motorcycle production
1953	61cid EL Panhead discontinued
1954	Harley-Davidson's golden anniversary celebrated with special 50th Anniversary Panhead
1958	**May** Elvis Presley appeared on the cover of *The Enthusiast*, sitting on a KH model
1958	Introduction of Duo-Glide with front and rear suspension
1965	Introduction of Electra-Glide with Panhead engine, electric start and 12 volt electrics
1969	AMF buys Harley-Davidson

1

Early Days
1903–1919

The history of the Harley-Davidson marque is both long and proud, but the beginnings of the now mighty company were distinctly humble. In the first years of the twentieth century Arthur Davidson and William S. Harley started work in their spare time on a single-cylinder motorcycle that displaced approximately 10 cubic inches (160cc). By 1903, with the assistance of Arthur's older brother Walter, they had a working motorcycle but it lacked hill climbing ability and required further development. The trio built two improved motorcycles in 1904 with the intention of selling them. The Davidson brothers' Aunt Janet pinstriped the

The founders of the Harley-Davidson company. From left to right: Arthur Davidson, Walter Davidson, William A. Davidson and William S. Harley. (HD)

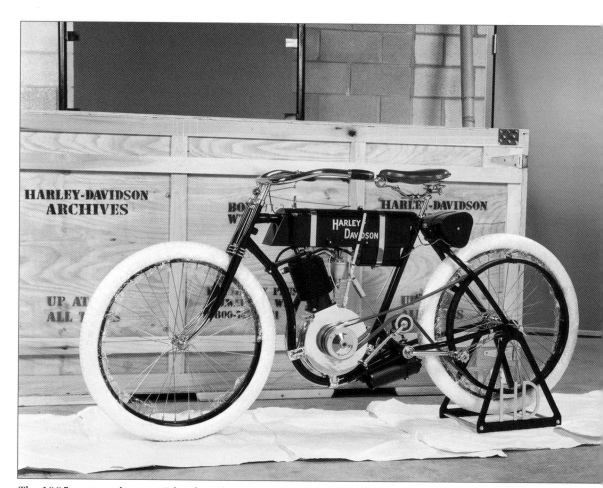

The 1905 motorcycles were F-head singles of 25 cubic inch (405cc) displacement in a bicycle-type diamond-style frame with belt drive and no brakes. ('F-head' denotes that the inlet valve was positioned in the cylinder head and the exhaust valve in the side of the cylinder.) The rider pedalled backwards to slow down. The machines were finished in black and featured numerous cycle-type components including the sprung saddle. (HD)

finished machines prior to their sale. From then on the company was in business and production increased exponentially; in 1905 – the year Walter Davidson became the first full-time employee of the fledgling concern – the group made 8 motorcycles, in 1906 it made 50, 150 in 1907 and more than 400 in 1908. The 1905 motorcycles were singles of 25 cubic inch displacement (405cc) in a bicycle-style frame with belt drive and no brakes. (The rider pedalled backwards to slow down.)

The first factory was a 10×15ft shed built by the Davidsons' father. In 1907 the third and oldest Davidson brother, William, also went to work for the company full time, and the firm was incorporated and sold shares. The two families retained a controlling portion of the stock until the company was sold to American Machine and Foundry (AMF) in 1969.

In April 1908 *Bicycling World and Motorcycle Review* summed up Harley-Davidsons in glowing terms: 'Of the latter day motorcycles, none so quickly earned a reputation as the Harley-Davidson. It is a machine the very appearance of which suggests substantiability and power, and its performance has borne out its appearance.' In June the same year Walter Davidson entered the Jack Pine Championship Endurance Run in the Catskill mountains and took first place, beating approximately sixty other entrants.

The Silent Gray Fellow was the first model produced in significant numbers by the workforce, which now numbered six. It was a single-cylinder machine and was named for its quiet running and optional grey paint scheme. The capacity of this four-stroke model was sequentially increased from 25 cubic inches (405cc) at its introduction to 30 cubic inches (500cc) in 1909 and then to 35 cubic inches (565cc) in 1913. Other changes made over the duration of the production run were to the design of the cylinder-head cooling fins and a reshaping of the front downtube of the steel loop frame. The gas tank was redesigned twice, in 1912 and 1916, while the belt drive was discontinued in 1914, being superseded by chain drive. Production of all singles was to end in 1918 as the general move towards V-twins was pursued by most American motorcycle manufacturers, including Harley-Davidson.

V-twin engines were seen as a way to increase the power of a motorcycle cheaply and the new engine design could easily be fitted into existing frames. Harley-Davidson's initial attempt at a V-twin had been introduced in 1909 but its first successful one emerged in 1911. This was soon followed by, a chain-drive version, the 8E. The 8E featured a 45 degree 61 cubic inch (1000cc) displacement V-twin and was introduced in 1912. The foundations for the company as it is today had been laid.

The Dawn of Racing

In 1909 a construction engineer, Jack Prince, who had built wooden velodromes, started construction of a larger wooden track for use by motorcycles in Los Angeles. It was named the Coliseum. Two riders, Jake De Rosier and Fred Huyck, came west from Chicago to race there. De Rosier, who was soon to become famous on the boards, set some speed records. Soon after, a board track built in Springfield, Massachusetts. It was also constructed by Prince but was partially financed by

By 1913 the popularity of belt final drive for motorcycles was waning and Harley-Davidson's V-twins, such as this Model 9, were equipped with chain final drive. These twins used a longer frame than the singles to allow the magneto to be located behind the engine. (GS)

Model	9	Power	8hp
Year	1913	Carburettor	Schebler
Engine type	inlet over exhaust (IOE) V-Twin	Top speed	65mph (105kph)
Displacement	61 cubic inches (989cc)	Frame	rigid, steel cradle
Bore and stroke	3.5×3.3 inches (89×84mm)	Forks	dual springs

George Hendee of the Hendee Manufacturing Company, makers of Indian motorcycles, to ensure a competition venue on Indian's home ground. The age of motorcycle racing as a mass spectator sport had arrived. Newspaper coverage was high and racing reports were filled with superlatives.

Particularly memorable board-track events of this period include the race between Charles 'Fearless' Balke and Ray Seymour at Elmhurst, California, over a distance of 50 miles. Balke rode for Excelsior and Seymour for Indian. The race was neck and neck for the entire distance, although Seymour took the win by a wheel length as he tried to overtake on the last lap. Board-track racing was a ruthless sport, dangerous for the participants. Jake De Rosier collided with a rider named Frank Hart at Guttenberg in New Jersey; De Rosier was not injured but Hart broke a leg. During a race at the Los Angeles Motordrome on 10 March 1912 worse luck awaited De Rosier who was riding an Excelsior and racing against Charles 'Fearless' Balke, also Excelsior mounted. De Rosier employed his usual tactic of slipstreaming a rider until he knew he could pull out and pass. Balke is reported to have looked over his shoulder as De Rosier made his move. Balke then seemed to lose control and swerved across De Rosier. The motorcycles collided, Jake De Rosier flew through the air and was thrown against the top fence of the track. The famous racer was severely injured and had to undergo two major operations in Los Angeles hospitals before he was well enough to return to Springfield to convalesce. During his period off the track De Rosier campaigned for improvements to the sport, including the introduction of rules requiring helmets and goggles for racers, regulations to keep novices and intoxicated riders off the tracks, and higher fences, although he would not live to see such things implemented. Still unwell almost a year after the accident, he had to undergo another operation. He died on 25 February 1913 from complications during surgery. His death shocked the American motorcycling world. In paying him tribute, one newspaper reporter wrote: 'There was but one Jake De Rosier, there will never be another, for the conditions under which he achieved fame will never return.' It was true: his death and the horrific deaths of six spectators and two riders – Ray Seymour and Indian rider Eddie Hasha – at a race in Newark, New Jersey, in September 1912 turned audiences away from the motordromes. The First World War, the rising cost of the timber used to build tracks and the oncoming Depression all contributed to the demise of board-track racing.

Accounts of the 1913 Denver, Colorado, Federation of American Motorcyclists Convention give an indication of what motorcycling was like in the early days. The decision to hold the convention in Denver was itself novel because this was the first time such an event had been run west of the Mississippi River. The meeting was hosted by the Colorado Motorcycle Club which had premises at the junction of Colfax Avenue and 14th Street. Motorcyclists began arriving in Denver on 21 July when forty riders from Chicago, Milwaukee and the Dakotas arrived late in the afternoon, having covered 125 miles from Stirling, Colorado, that day. A group numbering more than 130 arrived the next day from Kansas and the Southern States; they had been accompanied from Colorado Springs by members of the Colorado Motorcycle Club. Among this group was the President of the FAM, Dr E.J. Patterson, who had ridden in from his home in Pratt, Kansas, and six women riders on their own machines. One of these female riders was Patterson's daughter Inez,

Board-track racing was a dangerous game. The tracks were often badly maintained, the boards were soaked in oil from total-loss engine lubrication systems, some of the riders drank away their nerves and the racing was close – death and injury came suddenly and violently. This, and salacious press reports of goings-on at the tracks, led to a decline in the sport. This is a Chicago track photographed in 1920. (HD)

who was seventeen years of age; she had already made two motorcycle trips from Kansas to New York City accompanied by her father. On 23 July, another group of riders arrived but due to the poor condition of the roads in the Midwest after heavy rain, they had come by train with their bikes. Those riders already in Denver rode to the station to meet the train and it is estimated that in total 400 motorcycles paraded back to the clubhouse. The column was escorted by members of the Denver police department and featured in the *Denver Post*.

The experience of two stragglers from Kansas who also arrived in Denver on the 23rd gives an indication of how tough biking could be in America's vast open spaces. Harry Williams was an employee of the Pope company and had ridden his Pope motorcycle from Detroit to Hutchinson, Kansas, where he rendezvoused with the Kansas party. He then rode with them to Cannon City, Colorado, where another rider, Charles Pierce, also on a Pope motorcycle, had broken down. Williams had stayed behind to help fix the disabled machine. Both riders left for Denver twenty-four hours behind the main group and, intent on making up the lost time, rode through a severe thunderstorm. The pair crashed when a bolt of lightning struck the road immediately ahead of them. Both bikes were damaged but ridable and the they continued until the road became impassable within 10 miles of Denver. Williams and Pierce covered the last miles by riding between the rails of the Santa Fe railway track! Another motorcyclist with experience of riding in adverse conditions was also in Denver for the convention. Billy Teubner had been heralded as a hero in the Dayton, Ohio, flood in spring the same year after riding his motorcycle around the outlying areas of the town warning residents of the rising waters and giving alarms as the situation worsened. His actions allowed thousands to escape the flood. He had made Denver from Indianapolis in fourteen days. Another rider from Ohio – Jesse Campbell, Ohio commissioner for the FAM – had covered 1,700 miles in ten days, a respectable daily average given the condition of the roads.

The racing segment of the convention was scheduled for the weekend and noted competitors began arriving in Denver. Indian riders with factory support, Charles 'Fearless' Balke and Ray Seymour, were there to uphold the honour of the Springfield marque, while Red Armstrong flew the colours of Excelsior. A local rider – M.K. Fredericks, 'Curly' to his friends and fans – was among the favourites. There was controversy to come at the convention, though, as two tracks existed in Denver at the time: the mile dirt oval in Overland Park and the massive 3 mile board track at Tuileries Park. The popularity of board-track racing was then waning because of the dangers it posed to both riders and spectators. However, the Denver board track proprietors wanted the racing to run on their track. The FAM, on the other hand, wanted to run on the dirt. It was resolved that the championship would be decided on the dirt track. This was not the end of the dispute, however, as two of the best known figures in the fledgling motorcycle world were at odds over the issue of board-track racing. Dr J.P. Thornley of New York, Chairman of the FAM National Competitions Committee, was accused of siding with board-track race promoters by T.J. Sullivan, the Editor of *Motorcycling Magazine* at the assembly of the convention. Violence was only avoided because the meeting was firmly controlled from the chair by President Patterson. Later in the evening the two individuals accidentally met in the nearby Albany Hotel where a fight started. Other delegates present had to separate them. The various committees tried to resolve some of the problems and return some decorum to the proceedings. Finally, a compromise was reached: the official races would be held on Friday, Saturday and Sunday mornings on the dirt and an unofficial race would be held on Sunday afternoon on the board track. After this decision had been made, the evening's dance at the Colorado Motorcycle Club was generally acknowledged to have been a great success.

The next day saw elections for the FAM committee posts, and Patterson remained President. With the business of the convention resolved, the delegates went riding in the foothills of the Rockies, west of the city. Riders took in places such as Morrison, Golden, Lookout Mountain and Clear Creek Canyon.

The convention's racing programme was divided between amateur and professional events. Amateur and professional races for stock motorcycles were scheduled for Friday. A Brooklyn rider – John Constant – won the 1, 2, 5 and 25 mile races on a V-twin Indian averaging in excess of 60mph in each race. His time for the 25-miler was 24 minutes 14 seconds. During the 5 mile race the handlebars of his machine broke and he was forced to complete the event riding one handed. 'Fearless' Balke won the 5 and 10 mile professional races at a somewhat faster pace. Saturday's events got off to a delayed start because of rain but this had the beneficial effect of damping down the dust. The Manufacturers' Association Five-Mile Cup race was won by Will Feuerstein from Norfolk, Virginia, in 5 minutes 11 seconds. The professional 1-miler of the day saw a new record set by 'Fearless' Balke of 51 seconds dead. Later, the 10 mile professional race developed into a dice between Balke and Robert Perry from Chicago. In the last lap Balke's Indian started to misfire and Perry took the flag. Red Armstrong placed third. The Sunday morning programme included 5 and 10 mile professional races, both of which were also won by Robert Perry, who set a new record for 10 miles at 8.28. Soon afterwards the successful convention drew to a close.

Harley-Davidson's successful factory-backed racing efforts were to come slightly later.

A US Army Harley-Davidson sidecar outfit equipped with a machine gun being tested by the Wisconsin National Guard at a rifle range near the Milwaukee/Racine county line. The second outfit (behind) carries ammunition. Mud along the route had necessitated the removal of the front fenders of both machines. Harley-Davidson started supplying the US Army in 1917 and by the end of the First World War US forces had 14,666 Harley-Davidsons and 14,332 Harley-Davidson sidecars. (HD)

The First World War –

In 1913 Harley-Davidson sold 12,904 motorcycles and export sales began. The company engaged an Englishman, Duncan Watson, to arrange imports and sales in the UK and Europe. However, less than a year later the outbreak of the First World War brought a temporary end to exports to Europe and the trade was not resumed until 1919. The war did not directly involve the US until 1917 and in the meantime motorcycle racing gained enormously in popularity. Harley-Davidson riders scored victories at the 300 mile Dodge City Classics of 1915 and 1916 as well as the 300 mile race in Venice, California, the 200 mile event at Phoenix, Arizona, and the 150 mile event in Oklahoma City.

In 1915 Harley-Davidson introduced its first three-speed motorcycle, the Model 11-F. This machine was powered by the 60.34cid (988.83cc) V-twin engine that produced 11hp. It was fitted with a multiplate clutch and what Harley-Davidson described as a 'three-speed sliding gear transmission'. Gear changes were achieved with a foot-operated clutch pedal and a hand gear-lever. An automatic carburettor, Bosch magneto and a mechanically operated oil pump ensured engine reliability. The 11-F was assembled around a loop frame and its fuel tank and fenders were finished in grey, while other parts were nickel plated. Electric lights were an optional extra.

New for 1916 was the publication of *The Enthusiast*, Harley-Davidson's own magazine for its customers. *The Enthusiast* is still published and is the world's longest-running motorcycle magazine. In the same year Harleys were used in the border war with Mexican Pancho Villa, a known Indian rider!

The US became embroiled in the First World War in 1917 prompted by the sinking of the liner *Lusitania* that year and by the German policy of unrestricted submarine warfare. Before this date the US Army was still steeped in the cavalry traditions of fighting in the Old West; by the time the US became involved in the European conflict, the European nations were using tanks on the Western Front. The US Army caught up with mechanisation quickly and this meant that the war had a positive effect for Harley-Davidson. During the conflict the company supplied half its output of motorcycles to the US Army while at the same time preparing for postwar production and expansion of the factory. The company also set up a service school to train motorcycle mechanics for the Army. The school was retained after the war for educating Harley dealers' mechanics in factory techniques. Harley-Davidson entered the '20s on an optimistic note, with increasing sales of motorcycles and continuing development at its factory.

Company founders and fishermen William A. Davidson and William S. Harley, photographed in 1922, with a sidecar outfit manufactured by their company and the results of a good day's fishing. It is reported that the biggest 'walleye' on the string weighed 8.25lb. (HD)

The first Harley-Davidson factory was a shed built by the Davidsons' father. This was doubled in size in 1905 – as seen here – when Walter Davidson became the first full-time factory manager. By 1906 the company had a new building in Juneau Avenue, Milwaukee, where it remains to this day. (HD)

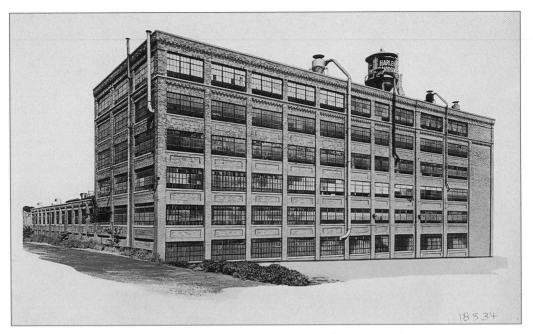

The brick-built Juneau Avenue factory. By 1910 the company had 150 employees, by 1911 almost 500, and around 1,000 in 1912. By 1920 it had the largest motorcycle factory in the world, at over 600,000 sq ft. (HD)

The inlet-over-exhaust belt-drive V-twin engine was first catalogued by Harley-Davidson in 1909, although an experimental one had been exhibited in 1907. The V-twin was not catalogued for 1910 but returned for 1911 as the Model 7 V-twin. This displaced 49.48 cubic inches and featured mechanical inlet valves. Chain final drive and a rear-hub clutch were first offered in 1912; 61cid V-twins were introduced in 1913. (HD)

William Ottaway, a former Thor motorcycles employee, took up a job with Harley-Davidson in 1914 to oversee the company's racing efforts through its new racing department. He is seen here aboard one of the inlet-over-exhaust models in 1924. (HD)

The Russian government ordered Harley-Davidson sidecar outfits in 1915 via Messrs Robertsons in London. The photograph above shows part of the order, while the one below pictures a single sidecar outfit with a Mr Korotkevick on the pillion seat. Korotkevick was the Russian government's representative in London at the time. (AC)

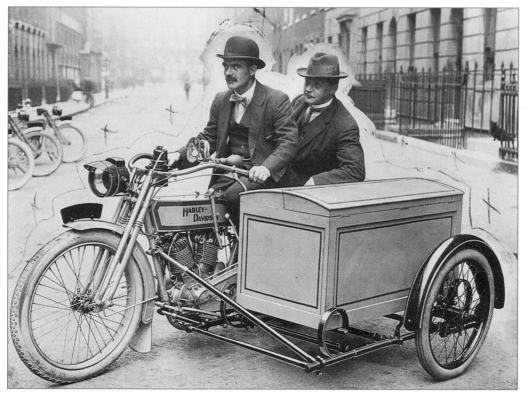

Harley-Davidson team racers on their bikes after winning the 1915 Dodge City 300 mile 'Cactus Classic' race. Left to right: Otto Walker (first), Harry Crandall (second), Joe Wolters (fourth), Leslie 'Red' Parkhurst (fifth), Spencer Stratton (sixth) and Ralph Cooper (seventh). The race attracted twenty-nine entrants on a range of Indian, Pope, Cyclone, Emblem, Excelsior and Harley-Davidson machines and was watched by 15,000 spectators. (HD)

A meeting of British motorcyclists in Richmond, Surrey, April 1915. Among the makes represented was Harley-Davidson – a Mr Hendreth of Strecklow rode in on this 6hp single-cylinder sidecar outfit. (AC)

One of several US Army colour postcards dating from the First World War that show military Harley-Davidsons, in this case a machine gun-equipped sidecar outfit in a military encampment. Postcards from the Second World War were printed from the US Army Signals Corps' black and white photographs. (AC)

A Harley-Davidson sidecar outfit in the foreground with two other makes of motorcycle during a tour of Ireland, 11 May 1916. (AC)

A snapshot of a Harley-Davidson outfit and riders taken on 13 July 1916. (AC)

Harley-Davidson's Model F was one of the motorcycles that established the company's reputation for the manufacture of V-twin engined machines. It was powered by a 45 degree F-head V-twin. The machines, including this one which was exported to India, featured a three-speed transmission, a redesigned oil pump and a rear-wheel brake. (BSH)

An F-head V-twin in India. This photograph was taken on 1 February 1917 and shows Percy Johnson who had just completed a tour of the Bengal coalfields on his Harley-Davidson sidecar outfit. He had covered 625 miles in eight days and had to contend not only with bad roads but also with a cyclone! (AC)

An unidentified girl aboard a Harley-Davidson single, Ireland, 1917. Also in the photograph are convalescing British soldiers who had been wounded in fighting during the First World War. The motorcycle has an Irish licence plate. (AC)

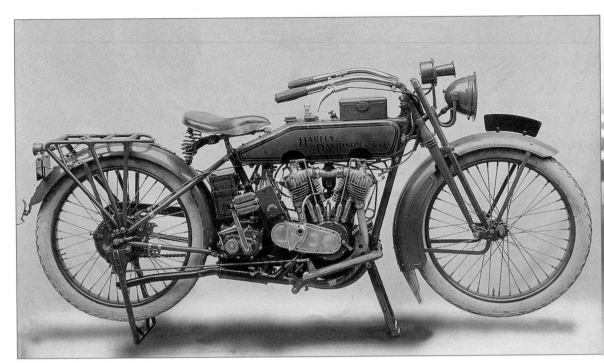

A 61cid (989cc) V-twin model fitted with Remy electric lights, 17 April 1919. By now the Harley-Davidson V-twins featured a three-speed chain-drive transmission with a foot-operated clutch pedal and a hand-operated gearshift, a configuration that remained standard for many years. This type of Harley also featured sprung forks, a type, albeit upgraded and strengthened, that endured until 1948. (AC)

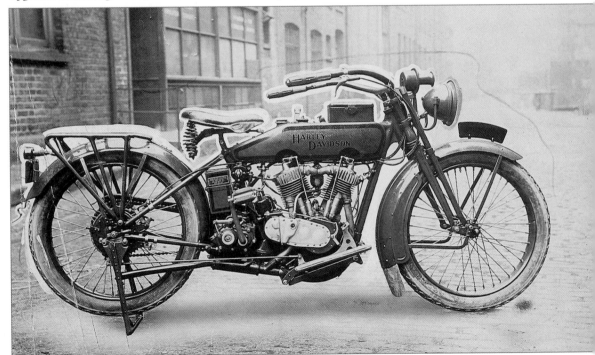

The 1919 61cid V-twins produced between 7 and 9hp and many were used for pulling sidecars. Olive green was a standard Harley colour at this time. Motorcycles that were not equipped with electric lights generally used acetylene ones back and front. Because the frames had no rear suspension, comfort for the rider came in the form of a sprung solo saddle. (AC)

2

The Roaring '20s

In the years immediately after the First World War Harley-Davidson exports to Europe resumed. Although the company suffered low sales in the early '20s as a result of competition from low-priced automobiles, it retained a strong export market, selling bikes in sixty-seven countries world-wide. The Harley-Davidson company, acknowledged as the biggest motorcycle manufacturer in the world, now embarked on a new programme to bolster sales around the globe. Employee Alfred Rich Child went to Cape Town, South Africa, and rode north the full length of the African continent on a J Model. *En route* he sold 400 motorcycles and established a number of new dealers. After this trip Child went to Japan and spent the next thirteen years importing Harley-Davidson motorcycles into the country. He also established a licensing agreement to enable Harleys to be made in Japan by a company called Rikuo.

Back in the United States, 1920 saw a record high in sales – 28,189 motorcycles. However, in 1921 sales were down more than 18,000 and for the first time the company made a loss. One of the reasons for this slump was competition from Ford's mass-produced car, the Model T, which was selling for almost the same price as a

This 1920 37cid Harley-Davidson uses an opposed twin-cylinder engine. While this configuration was commonly fitted by European manufacturers, Harley-Davidson generally used the V-twin engine type for its motorcycles. Much of the remainder of the bike, including the fenders and springer forks, is typical of other Harleys of the early '20s. This motorcycle was restored by a member of the Antique Motorcycle Club of America and once held the 'three flag' record. This involved riding between Canada, the US and Mexico and was a real challenge before the road network was developed. (AC)

sidecar outfit. At this time approximately 75 per cent of Harley-Davidson's machines left the factory equipped with sidecars.

Racing into Decline

Jim Davis won the 1920 Dodge City 300 mile race in 1920 and later the same year Ray Weishaar came first in a 200 mile event at Marion, Indiana. However, in some places the popularity of motorcycle racing took a downward turn in the early '20s. A number of racers' deaths were partially to blame. Bob Perry, who rode for Excelsior, was killed in an accident while testing an overhead camshaft racer at the Ascot Speedway in Los Angeles on 4 January 1920. Ignatz Schwinn cancelled all his Excelsior company's racing efforts immediately afterwards. Indian and Harley-Davidson were still involved, however, and set out to contest the 300 mile National in Dodge City on 4 July 1921. Indian had seven riders mounted on Franklin's Powerplus-derived race bikes, known as pocket-valves. Harley-Davidson entered Ralph Hepburn on an eight-valve machine and five other riders on twin-cam pocket-valve Harleys. A privateer, Waldo Korn, took part in the race on an Excelsior. The win in what was the last ever Kansas 300-miler went to Hepburn and Harley-Davidson. Soon afterwards the company temporarily retired from racing.

In 1921 Douglas Davidson (no relation), aboard a Harley-Davidson, became the first person to exceed 100mph on a motorcycle in Great Britain. He recorded a speed of 100.76mph at the Brooklands circuit.

The board-track phenomenon had not entirely passed and races were still being promoted. There were still enough reckless riders around who were prepared to risk all. Crowds continued to pay to watch their exploits and sample other attractions at the races – it has been reported that prostitutes openly solicited the crowds, illegal betting went on and bootleg liquor was to be found on sale. Understandably the transitory nature of the racers' lives and the excitement that the events brought to town encouraged uproarious behaviour. One group of racers who arrived in Chicago to race at the Riverview Park Motordrome are reported to have pooled their money and rented an entire brothel for the three days prior to the event! There are those who believe the danger of the board-track sport and its high accident rate led to motorcycling as a whole being perceived in a negative way and that this contributed to the decline in sales, especially when the press began referring to the motordromes as 'murderdromes'.

While Indian was still interested in promoting its motorcycles through racing, the impact of such promotion was lessened because neither the Harley-Davidson nor the Excelsior factories were taking part. Consequently, Indian reduced its budget for racing and competition motorcycling of this type went into decline. Charles Gustafson Jr oversaw the Indian team's efforts during this period. Albert 'Shrimp' Burns, Charles 'Fearless' Balke and Paul Bower, the latter too young to have earned a nickname, were all killed in separate racing accidents at Toledo, Hawthorne (Chicago) and Toledo respectively. Hill climb competition now began to increase in popularity and Indian riders achieved some endurance records. In 1922

HARLEY-DAVIDSON

The cover of Harley-Davidson's brochure from 1925. At this time motorcycling was still seen as an adventure for the young and affluent as the riders' attire suggests. Sidecars were very popular. (GS)

'Cannonball' Baker rode an Indian Scout from New York City to Los Angeles in 179 hours and 28 minutes. Over the 3,368 miles of the journey he used 40 gallons of gasoline and 5 gallons of lubricating oil. He averaged 20mph. The 300 mile National was held in Wichita, Kansas, in 1923 and was won by 'Curly' Fredericks on a 61cid Indian.

Bigger Capacities and the Model D

After the 1921 low, sales of Harley-Davidsons began to increase again, no doubt aided by the introduction that year of the first 74cid (1200cc) models. The large capacity of the new engine made it more suitable for pulling a sidecar and matched that of its major rival from Indian. This first 74cid engine was described as an F-head, a term which indicates the position of the inlet and exhaust valves; the inlet valve was in the cylinder head while the exhaust valve was in the side of the cylinder. The description of earlier engines as inlet-over-exhaust (IOE) models derives from the same source. The 74cid-powered Harley came in two versions: one featured a magneto and the other a generator, the FD and JD models respectively. The engine actually displaced 74.66 cubic inches (1207.1cc). Other developments followed through the '20s, including dual spring forks, speedometers, ammeters, new types of piston, better exhausts, a redesigned frame, a new style of fuel tank and front-wheel brakes.

Despite the general prosperity enjoyed by the USA in 1924 the year marked a still declining domestic market for motorcycles. Henderson Fours were being produced in small numbers, Ace was in serious financial difficulties and Excelsior had cut back its production. The main reason for the decline was nothing to do with bad publicity about racing or immoral behaviour at racetracks but simply the availability of the cheap mass-produced car. A Model T Ford was now cheaper than a sidecar outfit.

Law enforcement agency sales continued to be important to Harley-Davidson, Indian and other motorcycle manufacturers but these were not enough on their own. In 1925 Winston Churchill, Chancellor of the Exchequer in the Conservative government under Prime Minister Stanley Baldwin, levied a 33 per cent import tax against all foreign motorcycles. This pushed the retail price of American motorcycles so high that they became uncompetitive. Import taxes were introduced in the Australasian markets in 1929 as governments there sought to protect their domestic producers from cheap American goods.

By 1928 the JD and the smaller capacity model, the J, were available in higher performance versions; the JDL and JL were also fitted with front brakes for the first time. It was in this year that a new chapter opened in the history of Harley-Davidson: the company unveiled a new engine. It was a side-valve V-twin design that displaced 45 cubic inches (740cc) and was designated the Model D. However, it did not get off to the best of starts because of an unreliable gearbox and clutch, and the fact that it was only capable of 55mph. Production of the Model D was suspended in 1929 while the problems were resolved and it was reintroduced as 1930 in three guises – the D, DL and DLD. These three designations referred to the varying power outputs of the machines: 15, 18.5 and 20hp respectively. The D models featured a vertical generator at the front of the engine which earned them the slightly disparaging nickname of the 'three-cylinder Harley'.

The world economy took a turn for the worse when the Depression was heralded by the Wall Street Crash of 24 October 1929. It dealt most motor vehicle manufacturers, including Harley-Davidson, a severe blow and meant the '30s started less than optimistically for America as a whole.

In 1925 Harley-Davidson offered two twins of 61cid (1000cc) and two of 74cid (1200cc). These were the F and J, and FD and JD models respectively. The basic configuration of the engine was the same because they were all of an F-head V-twin type. All were supplied finished in olive green but there were further variations, including sidecar models and some with electric lights. Overall styling was now beginning to look more streamlined, particularly in the shape of the fuel tanks. (GS)

Olive green remained the standard factory colour for 1926 although optional hues – including grey – were made available around this time. The company was also working on side-valve configuration V-twins during this period and these would supersede the F-head types within two years. (GS)

Model	JD	Power	24hp
Year	1926	Carburettor	Schebler
Engine type	Flathead V-twin	Top speed	60mph
Displacement	74 cubic inches (1207cc)	Frame	rigid, steel cradle
Bore and stroke	3.4×4 inches (87×102mm)	Forks	spring

Initially Harley-Davidson was not interested in racing but became involved when the publicity value of wins on the track became clear. The company formed a racing department and built race bikes. For a period the racing machines were specially constructed with advanced multi-valve engines. Indirectly these expensive bespoke bikes led to the formation of the Class C system in the '30s which encouraged Harley's domination of the dirt track events. (HD)

The second generation of Davidsons, left to right: Gordon, Walter and Allan, photographed outside Dudley Perkins' dealership in San Francisco. Perkins is standing behind the bikes which are the so-called 'three-cylinders', the 1930 45cid side-valve V-twins. The three Davidsons were photographed during an 8,000 mile coast-to-coast trip in 1929. Gordon later became Production Manager for Harley-Davidson while Walter oversaw publicity and promotion. Allan did not join the company. (HD)

3
From Depression to War
1930–1939

The early '30s were characterised by the Depression which saw an estimated 13 million Americans out of work by 1932. It spelled the end of most of the remaining US motorcycle manufacturers. Excelsior could not withstand the pressure and closed in 1931, leaving Indian Motorcycles as Harley-Davidson's only domestic US competitor, but even these larger companies were lucky to survive this dark period in America's economic history. Harley-Davidson sales declined over the following years to an all time low of only 3,703 machines in 1933. Export sales had been hit by the 1929 introduction of higher import taxes in Australia and New Zealand.

The company resorted to desperate measures to attract customers – a wider choice of colours, extra chrome parts, optional accessories and even an extra wheel. In 1932 the Milwaukee company unveiled the Servicar, a three-wheeled machine powered by the 45 cubic inch side-valve engine. It was aimed at small businesses, garages and police departments. Garages used to send their mechanics out to breakdowns on Servicars, small businesses deployed them as delivery vehicles and policemen handed out parking tickets from them. The first Servicars featured the Model D engine although they were later upgraded in line with the solo 45 cubic inch (740cc) models.

The 1931 Harley-Davidson range brochure includes the 45cid (740cc) side-valve V-twin Model D, and the 30.50cid (500cc) single-cylinder Model C. The Model D was available as the D, DL, DLD, DC and DS, of which the latter was the sidecar machine. The Model C was available as the C, CH, CMG and CC. The smaller 21cid single, the larger V and variants were also produced at this time. The standard colour across the range was olive green although other colours were extra cost options. (GS)

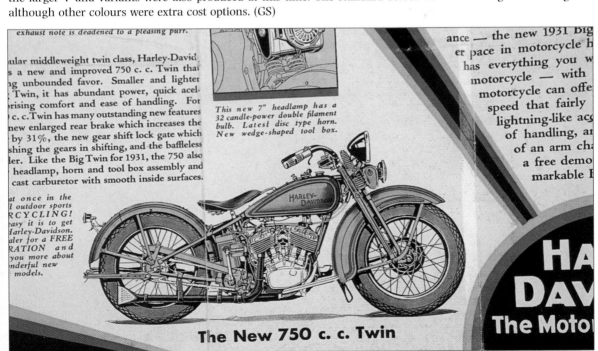

exhaust note is deadened to a pleasing purr.

...ular middleweight twin class, Harley-David... ...s a new and improved 750 c. c. Twin that ...ng unbounded favor. Smaller and lighter ...Twin, it has abundant power, quick acel- ...rising comfort and ease of handling. For ...c. c. Twin has many outstanding new features ...new enlarged rear brake which increases the ...by 31%, the new gear shift lock gate which ...shing the gears in shifting, and the baffleless ...ler. Like the Big Twin for 1931, the 750 also ...headlamp, horn and tool box assembly and ...cast carburetor with smooth inside surfaces.

...at once in the ...l outdoor sports ...RCYCLING! ...easy it is to get ...Harley-Davidson. ...aler for a FREE ...RATION and ...you more about ...nderful new ...models.

This new 7" headlamp has a 32 candle-power double filament bulb. Latest disc type horn. New wedge-shaped tool box.

...ance — the new 1931 Big ...er pace in motorcycle h ...has everything you w ...motorcycle — with ...motorcycle can offe ...speed that fairly ...lightning-like ac ...of handling, a ...of an arm ch ...a free demo ...markable

The New 750 c. c. Twin

HA DAV The Moto

43

The Enthusiast of August 1933 announced the 1934 range of Harley-Davidsons and trumpeted their new features, which included streamlined fenders, a new oiler, new pistons, a redesigned exhaust (the Burgess muffler) and a modern streamlined tank logo. The range included the 74cid 'Big Twin' VLD which produced 36bhp at 4600rpm and retailed at $310. The R model 45cid V-twin had a redesigned clutch and retailed at $280. The workaday three-wheelers, the G and GD Servicars, sold for $430; the two designations indicated the size of their rear bodies. (GS)

The Big Twins

In 1930 the new model Big Twins, designated V, were introduced and these were to put Harley-Davidson on the road to the success it enjoys today. The 74cid (1200cc) Model V was almost entirely new and shared few components with its F-head predecessor. The V models featured a side-valve engine where both inlet and exhaust valves were positioned alongside the cylinder bores. As a result the cylinder heads featured no moving parts and the engine type, regardless of maker, soon earned the nickname 'flathead', which soon became the term by which these models were differentiated from other Harleys. The cylinder heads were, of course, not completely flat; on the top they featured a number of cooling fins cast in during production and on their underside was a shaped combustion chamber. Each cylinder head was drilled and threaded for the spark plug.

The V Model was a four-stroke V-twin of 73.66cid (1207cc). It featured a three-speed transmission and was assembled around a steel loop frame. It had a total-loss lubrication system and was offered for sale in a number of guises of which the V and higher compression VL were two. These were followed by the magneto-equipped VM and VLM, as well as machines with varying compression ratios, the VS for sidecar work and the sporting VLD of 1934. The VLD featured a Y-shaped inlet manifold rather than the T-shaped one fitted to the earlier models. A larger displacement model was also available – the VLH, which displaced 80 cubic inches

45

Harley-Davidson's 1934 range brochure featured the same motorcycles as had been announced in *The Enthusiast* of August 1933 but presented them in a form designed to help dealers move them off the showroom floors. Including sidecar and sports versions, there were eight variants of the Model R offered and six variants of the VL, the Big Twin flathead. (GS)

(1340cc). Harley-Davidson used carburettors manufactured by Linkert and fitted a 1.25-inch M21 item to the VLD, which helped the engine produce 36bhp. While Harley-Davidson was still manufacturing total-loss lubrication engines its competitor Indian had advanced to dry-sump lubrication.

The Birth of the Knucklehead

The range of 45cid D models were redesignated the R, RL and RLD in 1932 when the generator was repositioned and the pistons were redesigned along with the oil pump, flywheels and clutch. The R series later became the W models but the next major step for Harley-Davidson was to be the introduction of overhead valves.

Parallel to the development of the various side-valve engines, the Milwaukee factory produced an overhead-valve design which went into production in 1936, providing better gas flow and combustion. It was designated the 61E Model – the 61 equated to its displacement in cubic inches (1000cc). The engine soon became known as the Knucklehead because of its rocker covers' resemblance to the knuckles of a clenched fist. The Knucklehead was the first Harley to have dry-sump lubrication – oil recirculates between the oil tank and engine – instead of a total-loss system. The horseshoe-shaped oil tank was located under the seat. The engine was fitted into a double loop frame and a new style of gas tank appeared. It was made in halves, hid the frame tubes and had the speedometer set into a dash plate that fitted between the two pieces. Despite the advanced engine much of the remainder of the machine was typical of Harley-Davidsons of the time. The frame was of the rigid type with no rear suspension; rider comfort was provided by means of a sprung saddle and the forks were still of the springer design.

The EL model was soon in the news when Joe Petrali rode one to various speed records on the sands of Daytona Beach in Florida. Petrali briefly rode Indians but then became one of Harley-Davidson's star riders, winning the National Championship on a Harley 1925. He was born in San Francisco in 1904 and had become interested in motorcycles as a boy. His first machine was a belt-driven Flanders which he bought when he was twelve. In 1920 he purchased a second-hand Indian from Jud Carriker's dealership in Santa Ana, California. On this he raced against the powerful Harley team at the Fresno, California, board track. The Harley riders boxed him in but he fought his way out and took second place. This ride earned him a place – on a borrowed Harley – in another big race. He won and as a result secured a position in the Harley-Davidson team. When Harley temporarily retired from racing in 1921, Petrali obtained a ride with Excelsior. On an Excelsior he broke three national speed records while qualifying for an event in Altoona, Philadelphia. He also won the main 20 mile race of the event on 9 July 1926. When Excelsior left motorcycle racing Petrali went back to Harley-Davidson with whom he stayed throughout the Depression. In 1937 he rode the new Knucklehead on Daytona Beach to a record – previously held by an Indian machine. Petrali's Knucklehead-powered motorcycle was clocked at 136.183mph, an American speed record and a world record for a non-supercharged-engined motorcycle. Later Petrali retired from racing altogether; he worked on Indianapolis Cars and was then employed by the eccentric industrialist Howard Hughes. Petrali flew with Hughes in the one and only test flight of the Spruce Goose, Hughes' massive flying boat, at Long Beach, California.

The Knucklehead was available as a 61 cubic inch (1000cc) machine from 1936 (the year the company became unionised). It was designated the 61E, while the 74 cubic inch (1200cc) model produced from 1941 was the 61F. It is generally accepted that the 61E was the model from which current Harley-Davidsons draw their styling.

The Introduction of Class C

As the US emerged from the depths of the Depression motorcycling again became a popular pastime. American motorcycle sport had been in the doldrums and in an

The EL Knucklehead was introduced in 1936. It was Harley-Davidson's first overhead-valve Big Twin V-Twin and gained the Knucklehead nickname because of the distinctive shape of the rocker covers. This is a 1937 model and for that year the air intake was changed to the one seen here and the frame was strengthened. The art deco-style 'comet' tank logo was used from 1936 to 1939 inclusive. (GS)

Model	EL	Power	40hp
Year	1937	Carburettor	Linkert
Engine type	overhead valve V-twin 'Knucklehead'	Top speed	95mph
Displacement	61 cubic inches (989 cc)	Frame	rigid, steel cradle
Bore and stroke	3.31×3.5 inches (84×89 mm)	Forks	springer

attempt to revitalise it the AMA's Class C was born. To be raced in Class C a bike could displace no more than 45 cubic inches (750cc) and would normally have two cylinders and side valves, simply because that was the spec that the big American factories – Harley and Indian – offered the man in the street through their dealers. The idea was to stop the few wealthy teams with exotic, specially constructed engines winning everything.

Class C was a great success and led to the enduring fame of events like the Daytona 200. It also ensured that dirt-track bikes were based on the venerable 'sidestick' 45 cubic inch (750cc) Harleys and Indians and that every town had a dirt oval. The establishment of Class C gave motorcycle racing a wider appeal; 'ordinary' riders could compete without having to run expensive specialist race bikes. This and the staging of a number of AMA-sanctioned 100 and 200 mile National races in places like Savannah, Georgia, and Daytona ensured that races started to attract huge crowds of spectators. Many riders emulated the style of the mildly modified race bikes for street use – Class C rules meant that race bikes were required to be street legal prior to the race. As a result, motorcycles that can be termed pre-war customs were usually bikes which had been modified by cutting down or removing the front fender and bobtailing – later shortened to bobbing – the rear fender. Sometimes a front fender was fitted to the back with the flared trailing end positioned much further around the wheel than normal and a pillion pad fitted, the whole being supported by an adapted or specifically fabricated fender strut. These modifications were made to both Harley-Davidson and Indian motorcycles reflecting the fact that both were popular American bikes and that much of the racetrack rivalry was between the motorcycles of the two companies. Racing in particular and motorcycling in general were to be curtailed when the US entered the Second World War following the Japanese air strike against Pearl Harbor in December 1941.

Despite the introduction of the overhead-valve EL models in 1936 the company did not abandon its production of side-valve big twins. In 1937 the V model range was redesignated U, UL and ULH as it was upgraded to dry-sump lubrication. The smaller capacity V-twins were also converted to dry-sump lubrication and redesignated the W, WL and WLD. The WLD was a sports version of the WL, but the WL would become famous in its military guise as the WLA and WLC after it was adopted by the armed forces of several Allied nations.

Vice President of the company, William A. Davidson, died on 21 April 1937. The decade drew to a close as the clouds of war again gathered in Europe although in domestic racing Harley-Davidson finished the '30s on a high. In the Oakland, California, 200 race held on 1 October 1939 Harley-Davidson riders Jack Cottrell and Armando Magri placed first and second respectively. Both riders were on WLDR models, the racing version of the WLD.

Winners of first place in the Atlanta, Ga., 24-Hour Race. William Bracy, standing, and O. C. Hammond in saddle of stock 45 Harley-Davidson with which they piled up 1366 miles.

24 Hour Race
won by HARLEY-DAVIDSON

Bert Baisden and his 1934 Harley-Davidson with which he and his team-mate scored second with a total of 1359 miles.

Third place winner, Jack Roberts, who with his relief rider, made a total of 1313 miles in the grind around the clock.

ATLANTA, Georgia, July 15— In one of the most grueling and hardest fought races ever staged in the history of motorcycling, Harley-Davidson riders captured the first five places in the 24-Hour Race held on the historic one-mile Lakewood dirt track.

William Bracy, piloting a '33 stock 45 Harley-Davidson and relief rider, O. C. Hammond, captured first place with the stupendous total of 1366 miles — an average of nearly 57 miles per hour. A close contender most of the race, Bert Baisden, on a '34 stock 45 Harley-Davidson and relief rider, Todd Haygood, rolled up 1359 miles. Jack Roberts, on a '33 stock 45, and Harley Taylor, as relief rider, came in third with 1313 miles. Lt. Ronnie Wilson of the Augusta, Ga., Police Department came in fourth and George Gunn, Atlanta, fifth.

A furious pace was set in the race right from the start. Baisden made the first one hundred miles in eighty-eight minutes. All the time these riders handled the throttle as though they were in a twenty-five mile race instead of a twenty-four hour grind. It was a marvelous exhibition of the ability of the riders and an outstanding demonstration of the staunchness and the stamina of the Harley-Davidson motorcycles.

Harley-Davidson Motor Co., MILWAUKEE U. S. A.

RIDE A WINNER

William Bracy and O.C. Hammond won the 1933 24-hour race held in Atlanta, Georgia, riding a stock 1933 Harley 45. They covered 1,366 miles in the allotted period. In second place were Bert Baisden and Todd Haygood and in third were Jack Roberts and Hank Taylor, all on Harley-Davidsons. (GS)

The Big Twin flathead was a magnificent Harley-Davidson at the time of its introduction in 1930 and it remained an important model in the company's range until it was replaced by the Model U in 1937. There were numerous versions of the Model V including both 74 and 80cid models as well as annual detail upgrades. The latter included various changes of tank logo and rear light. The bike seen here has the 'airflow' tail-light, for example. (HD)

During the '30s the US Army acquired Harley-Davidson 45cid motorcycles, beginning with the R models in 1932. These were followed by RL models in 1934 and WL models in 1937. This is a WL. The original caption for the picture said: 'Harold Holdem of Troop A 1st Reconnaissance Squadron. He is equipped with a Thompson submachine gun used for the protection of a despatch rider carrying confidential messages from Army Headquarters during recent maneuvers of the First Cavalry Division of the US Army.' The US Army was preparing for conflict despite not being involved in the Second World War from its outbreak. (IWM)

The *Enthusiast* of October 1937 previewed the 1938 models, which included 45cid flathead twins, 61cid ohv Knuckleheads, 74 and 80cid flatheads, Servicars and sidecars. In the news it was reported that William Muehlenbeck Jr of Saginaw, Michigan, had won the 13th Jackpine Endurance Run, a noted motorcycling competition of the time, on a 1937 Harley-Davidson 45. (GS)

BOY, THESE ARE MOTORCYCLES !— . . . . . THE GREATEST OF ALL HARLEY-DAVIDSONS

The 1938 Models

★ Red and Green Signal Lights for Oil Pressure and Generator Charge ★ Shaved Timing Gears on All Models ★ Completely Enclosed Rocker Arm Assembly on 61 OHV ★ Larger Oil Return Pipes in 61 OHV Valve Spring Covers ★ Interconnected Brake Shoes in Service Brakes on Big Twins ★ Improved Transmission Gears and Shifter Clutches in All Models ★ Oil Leakage Minimized in Valve Cover System on 45, 74, 80 ★ Shifting Mechanism on 45 Twins Same Type as Big Twins ★ Larger and More Efficient Burgess Muffler on Servi-Car ★ Timing Gears on 45, 74, 80 Models Now Run in Oil Bath ★ Compression-type Oil Pipe Connections on All Models ★ Rock-under Clutch Pedal Now Incorporated on 45 Twin ★ Frames Greatly Strengthened on 61, 74, and 80 Models ★ Speedometer Dial Features Easily Read Calibrations ★ Self-aligning Lower Head Cone on Big Twins ★ Larger Clutch Thrust Bearing on All Models ★ New Striping and Beautiful Color Options ★ Larger Oil Vent Pipes on Big Twins ★ Zerk-Alemite Fittings on All Models ★ Enclosed Rear Chain on Servi-Car ★ New Jaw-type Clamp on Servi-Car

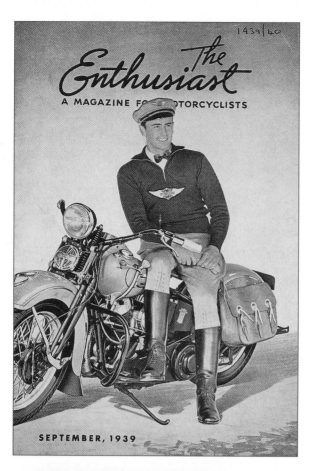

SEPTEMBER, 1939

In the September 1939 edition of *The Enthusiast* Harley-Davidson announced a new range of 1940 motorcycles. The bikes that 'have what it takes' included the 45, 74 and 80cid side-valve V-twins and the 61cid EL Knucklehead, pictured in the magazine and on its cover with a rider in typical motorcycle club attire of the time. The ohv Knucklehead was the top-of-the-range machine because of its advanced engine but styling of the mudguards, tanks and trim was similar across all models. The bikes were all based around rigid frames and springer forks. (GS)

THEY'VE GOT WHAT IT TAKES!

The 1940 MODELS

★ Instant Gas Reserve Valve ★ Streamlined Footboards ★ Chrome Nameplates ★ Ribbed Crankcases on Big Twins ★ Speedlined Tool Box on Big Twins ★ Tubular Front Fork on 45 and Servi-Car ★ Deep-finned Aluminum Heads Standard on 80 Twins and 45 WLD, Available on 74 ★ Front Forks Heat Treated ★ Improved Oil Distribution in Cylinders of 45, 61, and Servi-Car Motors ★ New Big Twin Crank Pin and Rollers ★ Cast Front Wheel Brake Drums on Big Twins and Servi-Car Rear Wheels ★ More 61 OHV Horsepower ★ Transmission and Clutch Improvements ★ Copper-flange Terminals ★ Improved Interchangeable Wheel Hubs ★ 5.00" x 16" Tires and Rims Available ★ New Saddle-top Leather ★ Many Servi-Car Advancements ★ Vertical Rod Antenna and Improved Vibrator on Radio Police Model ★ New Accessory Groups ★ New Color Scheme, New Striping and Beautiful Color Options ★ Lower Prices.

HARLEY-DAVIDSON

Swing into the saddle... Let a ride decide!

4

The Second World War

The outbreak of the Second World War in Europe did not affect the production of civilian motorcycles for the US domestic market but the Japanese air strike of December 1941 against Pearl Harbor in Hawaii did.

The 1940 range of Harley-Davidson solo motorcycles included the 45, 74 and 80cid side-valve twins and the 61cid ohv twin. Several of the side-valve variants came with aluminium-finned cylinder heads which offered improved performance. Styling, based around springer forks and rigid frames, was similar across the range and included a new tank badge for all models.

A slightly upgraded civilian motorcycle range was announced in the autumn of 1940 for 1941, while the company further developed its military WL models. Production of civilian motorcycles was suspended almost immediately after the attack on Pearl Harbor as industrial companies such as Harley-Davidson turned their production lines over to the war effort. The military specification WLs were produced in large numbers along with a tiny number of other models for the police and for 'essential use'.

Preparing for War

The US made preparations for war almost as though it was inevitable that the country would become embroiled in the conflict. Mechanisation of the US Army's cavalry units began in the late '30s but it was not until 1940 that funds were available to procure sufficient equipment to complete the process. Harley-Davidson sought to supply motorcycles to the Army and shipped some WL models to Fort Knox – more famous as the nation's bullion depository – for evaluation by the Mechanized Cavalry Board. The company received small contracts to supply motorcycles, as did Indian. Harley-Davidson was to provide the WLA – a military version of the WL.

The Canadian military also ordered motorcycles. Canada became involved in the Second World War before the USA and a machine designated the WLC was specifically built for its servicemen. The A suffix indicates an Army specification machine while the C suffix denotes a Canadian Army motorcycle. Military WLs were also supplied to Britain, Russia, Australia and South Africa.

The WLA and C were assembled around a steel loop frame and were powered by an engine with a capacity of 45.12 cubic inches which gave the four-stroke twin a top speed of 65mph. It produced 23bhp at 4600rpm and used a three-speed transmission. The two models differed only in details and were used all around the world during the war years. In the years after 1945 they became

WLA Harley-Davidsons, such as this restored example, were built for the US Army during the Second World War. The machines were based on the pre-war WL models but were equipped to a military specification that included oil bath air filters, a rear rack, holster, military lights and a lack of chrome. Minor changes were made during the wartime production run – for example, mudguards were made using less steel and rubber parts were minimised. This bike has the last-produced type of military mudguards. (GS)

Model	WLA	Power	23.5hp
Year	1942	Carburettor	Linkert
Engine type	Flathead V-twin	Top speed	60mph
Displacement	45 cubic inches (739cc)	Frame	rigid, steel cradle
Bore and stroke	2.75×3.8 inches (70×97mm)	Forks	springers

Harley-Davidson built the WLC version of the military WL for the Canadian Army. The 1942 WLC, seen here being used by Corporal R. Power of the Canadian Provost Corps for military traffic duties, diverged from the WLA in details. Differences include the distinctive blackout lamps fitted to both back and front fenders as well as the front stand and additional toolbox fitted on the front mudguard. Unlike the WLA models, the motorcycle has no rear luggage rack. (IWM)

popular as cheap civilian transport left behind by the US Army and popularised Harley-Davidsons in countries where the American machines were not widely available.

A reorganisation of the US Army was now under way and involved the creation of a new divisional structure. Each division was to consist of three independent infantry regiments and support units with enough transport to move regiment-sized groups. Reconnaissance troops would ride 'point' at the front of the division. These soldiers were intended to be mobile and were equipped with a variety of trucks and motorcycles. Of the latter there were eight solos and three combinations per troop. Unlike the German Army which had machine gun-armed sidecar outfits, the US Army basically saw the motorcycle as a replacement for the horse, the idea being that motorcycles would carry scouts forward from where dismounted scouting could be carried out. This structure was quickly modified as other technology became available. The Willys Jeep, which was introduced in 1941, soon relegated motorcycles to service tasks away from the fighting. They became the reliable workhorses of despatch riders, military policemen and convoy escorts, and so stayed in sufficient demand for Harley-Davidson to continue building military motorcycles for the duration of the war.

The WLA and WLCs changed slightly from year to year as refinements were made. For example, rubber parts were reduced to cope with the short supply of the commodity after numerous Japanese conquests in South-East Asia. Harley-Davidson made approximately 88,000 motorcycles during the war years and a large percentage of these were supplied to the other Allied nations. The factory received a number of accolades for its efforts, including an Army/Navy E for Excellence award. This was presented at a ceremony at the factory on 12 May 1943.

During the war years Harley-Davidson also produced a number of flat-twin-engined motorcycles – the XA – at the request of the US government and contributed to a number of other military projects that did not progress beyond the prototype stage. Two of the founders died during the war years, Walter Davidson in February 1942 and William S. Harley in September 1943.

Ploughing through Mudholes

In *The Brass Ring* the noted Second World War cartoonist Bill Mauldin recalled his wartime motorcycling experiences on a WLA in Italy with the US 45th Infantry Division: 'I went to a big ordnance depot in Naples and asked if they had a couple of motorcycles which had run over mines or been mashed by shells. What I had in mind was putting together the halves of two machines which had been hit in different places. I hadn't grown up hanging around those two mechanical geniuses, my father and brother, for nothing.

"Hell we hardly ever get anything that was busted in combat," the man at the junk pile told me. "Usually it's drunk driving." I not only got the germ of a cartoon idea from this, but also ended up with a slightly bent Harley-Davidson which I was told had run under the back of a truck, leaving its rider plastered on the tailgate. The ordnance boys lent me some tools and I got the thing running all right, though it crabbed slightly. During the next couple of weeks, I made two trips to the 45th on my bike. I would have kept on this way, except as I became a better rider I couldn't resist becoming a smart-ass. I would retard the spark going downhill to make backfires, squirrel my way through convoys, and plow through mudholes at high speeds. One of these finally trapped me. It was an old bomb crater full of water.'

Two members of the Minneapolis police department aboard their Big Twin flathead Harley-Davidsons. The tank badges identify these as 1940 models. The motorcycles have a number of items of police equipment, including flashing lights either side of the springs of the springer forks and sirens beside the rear wheels. It is this magnificent styling that Harley-Davidson has sought to preserve right up to the present. (HD)

The March 1940 edition of *The Enthusiast* was able to report on Rhode Islander Babe Tancrede's win in the 1940 Daytona 200, the ninth running of the 200-miler and the last prior to the US becoming involved in the Second World War. There were sixty-eight starters in the race and the magazine was pleased to report that of the fifteen finishers, twelve were riding 45 cubic inch Harleys. Other news in this issue was typical of the era: Florence Sky had ridden her 1935 45 on a tour of Mexico; the police departments of both Kalamazoo and Racine were using the three-wheeled Servicars for traffic duties; news had been received from twenty-four clubs in twelve US states. (GS)

The original caption for this photograph reads: 'A Canadian motorcyclist finds himself the centre of attention in the grounds of an English country house that was used as a brigade HQ.' This 1942 WLC is additionally equipped with a British-style pillion seat, often referred to as a tandem seat. The passenger footrests and brackets take the place of the rear crash-bar. (IWM)

Originally the US Army intended to use eight solo motorcycles and three sidecar outfits to ride 'point' ahead of its armoured divisions. These reconnaissance units were also intended to use White scout cars and Dodge 4×4s but the advent of the Jeep changed the numbers and types of vehicles used. This photograph, taken in New Caledonia in October 1942, shows early 'slat grille' Willys MB Jeeps with White scout cars and Harley-Davidsons. (AC)

By December 1942 the US had been in the war for a year and in its own bit of morale boosting *The Enthusiast* featured on its cover an early WLA motorcycle (it has longer forks than the later versions) which belonged to the Armored Force School at Fort Knox, Kentucky. Inside, the school was featured in detail, including its workshops, off-road riding course and an experimental XA flat-twin motorcycle. Another article featured Camp Roberts, a replacement training centre in California where the MPs rode WLA and XA Harleys. The club news section was packed with reports from 'the boys in the service'. (GS)

The Enthusiast

A MAGAZINE FOR MOTORCYCLISTS
DECEMBER 1942

Opposite: A line up of WLA 45s similar to the one in the picture at the top of page 63, except for the fact that these bikes have windshields fitted. The photograph shows: 'Lieutenant Howard T. Chase briefing US Army motorcycle police before they take off on a day's manoeuvres'. The windshields, horns, leg shields, crash-bars and the leading edge of the fenders have been painted white and some of the numbered bikes have other details. No. 11 has crossed pistols painted on the windshield and no. 1 has its windshield stencilled with the name Donna. Who she was can only be guessed. (IWM)

The original official caption to this photograph reads: 'Rough riding US Army military police toughen up on practice riding pits in Britain for the tougher job ahead, to prevent supplies and men piling up in confusion on beach heads when the Allied attack on Nazi-held Europe starts.' The motorcycles are WLAs. (IWM)

The original caption to this picture of an airborne WLA stated that: 'A motorcycle rider of only two months, Pvt Wilburn L. Cummings flies high over a shell hole obstacle somewhere in England. The course is designed to acquaint riders with conditions similar to those they expect to face under combat.' The photograph clearly shows the Oakes oil bath aircleaner behind the rider's leg which was a military specification component. (IWM)

Opposite: A portrait of the rider of a US Army WLA head on during a training exercise. (IWM)

The liberation of Europe had yet to start but the Allies conquered the Axis forces in North Africa in 1943 after the Battle of Kasserine Pass. Here General Von Arnim is taken prisoner by the British watched by a curious American MP on a WLA. The second representative of Hitler's 'master race' (extreme right) seems incredulous that an African-American is among his captors. (IWM)

Private First Class Carl Sturdevant seen on a WLA with his surname stencilled on the windshield was among the MPs charged with escorting convoys through London. The wartime censor has obliterated much of his unit's markings from the front fender of his bike. The WLA's headlamp lens has been partially painted to reduce the light emitted during the blackout. Just visible behind the car are US Army Dodge and GMC vehicles. (IWM)

Opposite: When this photograph was taken Private Jacob Zuideme and Private First Class William Foster were US Army MPs employed in guiding US Army convoys through London. Their Harleys are standard WLA models, although they are not equipped with the rifle scabbard and ammunition box that were designed to be attached to the front forks. It is also interesting to note that the motorcycle in the foreground has been fitted with a non-standard blackout headlamp. (IWM)

A lengthy line-up of US Army WLAs in London in front of a building where a US Army 'snowdrop' is manning the entrance. The motorcycle nearest the camera is completely devoid of a headlamp but still has its blackout lamps fitted. The white panel painted on the front fender of each bike was designed to make them more visible to other road users during the blackout. (IWM)

An M10 tank destroyer – a 3-inch gun mounted on a Sherman M4 chassis – passes through Percy, France, on 1 August 1944 following the successful American breakout from the Normandy beach heads. In the foreground is a 1942 WLA, presumably an MP's bike. It has the standard military fittings, including rifle holster and ammunition box on either side of the forks, crash-bars, twin military tail-lights and stencilled US Army markings. (AC)

Opposite: The 2nd French Division was part of the US 3rd Army between 1 August 1944 and 9 May 1945. This motorcycle unit is part of the 2nd French Division, indicated by the emblem – the outline of France with the Cross of Lorraine – on the windshield of the Harley nearest the camera. The unit is waiting to board a ship in an English seaport. Chalked across the windshield is the boarding information including LST 433, the number of the landing ship about to transport the unit. The motorcycle without a windshield has the same information on its headlight. (IWM)

In late July 1944 the US Army launched a major offensive to enlarge the area of France under its control. Part of this action included a push for the town of Coutances, during which this atmospheric photograph was taken. It shows Sergeant Joseph A. De Marco of New York City (at left in leather jacket) getting information from American military policemen stationed at a crossroads in Les Champs de Losque. One of the MPs sits astride a WLA; the unit markings on its front fender have been partially obscured by the photographic censor, but it is possible to ascertain that the Harley belonged to the 1st US Army and was the forty-first vehicle of an A Company. (IWM)

The Royal Air Force (RAF) used some WLC Harley-Davidsons, including this one which was about to leave Creully, north-west of Caen in Normandy, in July 1944. Clearly illustrated here is one of the differences between the WLC and WLA: the WLC uses a big-twin-type front brake while the WLA was fitted with a front hub that featured an integral brake drum. (IWM)

The US Army in Australia. The original caption suggested that special squads of motorbike troops were being trained at a US camp in Australia and that the rider tore up to position at 35mph, leapt off and was in action with a Thompson submachine gun in 3 seconds. The standard US military tail-lights fitted from 1942 onwards are clearly visible. The registration number suggests that the bike was one of a batch of 4,258 1942 WLAs supplied to the US Army. (IWM)

A US Army despatch rider collects a message from an English Tommy at a typewriter while another GI uses the field telephone. The leg-shields seen fitted to this US Army WLA were an 'accessory part'. Units sprayed white five-pointed stars on to their own bikes so the exact size of the star, its position and quality of the work varied. Here a star is sprayed on both gas tank and leg-shields, and the overspray is clearly visible. The bracket for a rifle scabbard is fitted but is devoid of both leather scabbard and gun. (AC)

A convoy of US Army staff cars escorted by a trio of riders mounted on WLA Harley-Davidsons. Note that the white painted lettering on the windshields varies and that while one Harley has a rifle in place in its scabbard, the others do not. The headlamps are not blacked out. (AC)

5
The Postwar Boom
1946–1954

After the end of the Second World War Harley-Davidson resumed civilian production. The company initially reintroduced the motorcycles from its pre-war range to satisfy pent up demand from returning servicemen while it prepared new and updated models. The 1947 EL and FL Knuckleheads were among the pre-war machines that were reintroduced, and were almost the last of the Knuckleheads. Close scrutiny of the pre- and postwar Knuckleheads reveals a number of styling changes that were made for the 1947 model year. Between 1936 and 1946 Harley-Davidson had fitted a rounded tail-light but it was superseded by a new design for the 1947 bikes. In the way Harley parts acquire nicknames to differentiate them, the new and old tail-lights came to be referred to as the beehive and the tombstone respectively. Other changes made at the same time included a shift from the 'cat's-eye' dash cover to a more modern-looking one, now known as the 'two-light' dash because much later it was superseded by the 'three-light' dash. The cat's-eye and two-light descriptions refer to the type of ignition and oil warning lights used adjacent to the speedometer. Front fender lights were changed and in place of the manually adjusted ride control a hydraulic damper was fitted.

Postwar shortages of raw materials initially caused difficulties for the resumption of civilian motorcycle production but gradually these were overcome and work got back to normal. After 1945 the 45 cubic inch flathead models, including the three-wheeler Servicar, were also reintroduced in almost pre-war form – once again the fenders were valanced, the diameter of the wheels was reduced to 16 inches from the 18 inches of military wheels, and chromed parts returned. There were upgrades to the model; the tail-light and dash covers were redesigned and matched those to be found on other models in Harley-Davidson's postwar range. The flathead WL solos were discontinued in 1952 but production of the same 45 cubic inch flathead engine continued as the power plant for the three-wheeler G and GA Servicars, which were manufactured until 1973.

The Arrival of the Panhead

In the years immediately after the Second World War ex-army Harley-Davidsons were sold to transport-hungry civilians around the world. In the USA new bikes which had not been delivered to the Army went on sale, while in other countries including Holland and France Harleys left behind by the Allied forces went on sale.

Many owners, of course, preferred to repaint their old army machines and fit chromed parts and accessories. Some of these machines were so well refurbished that it is hard to tell them apart from genuine civilian models.

The Knuckleheads were superseded in 1948. Technology had progressed and a new overhead-valve Harley-Davidson Big Twin engine was unveiled. It arrived to critical acclaim and was quickly referred to as the Panhead because, as the slang name implies, its rocker covers look like upturned cooking pans. The 74cid (1200cc) capacity four-stroke twin produced 55bhp and was capable of a top speed of 102mph with a four-speed transmission. The Panhead motor essentially comprised a new top end on the existing Knucklehead bottom end. The cylinder heads were cast from aluminium because there had been problems with the all-iron Knucklehead, hydraulic lifters contributed to a quieter running engine and a larger oil pump was used to improve lubrication. The Panhead models superseded the Knucklehead ones but the new motorcyles retained the E and F designations for the 61 and 74 cubic inch versions.

Improvements to the Big Twins did not end there: soon the cycle parts of the bike were also upgraded. For one year only – 1948 – Harley-Davidson marketed a Panhead-engined motorcycle that featured a rigid frame and springer forks. Because of this short production run so-called 'springer pans' are collectable motorcycles.

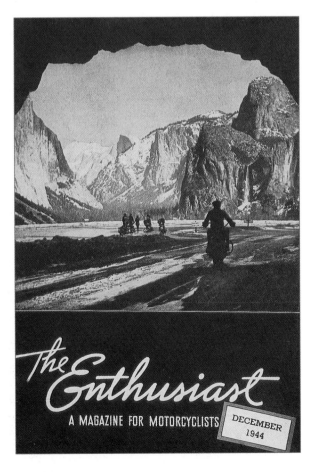

The Enthusiast of December 1944, published while the US Army was engaged in the Battle of the Bulge, featured Tom Henry of Stockton, California, on its cover, riding through the Yosemite National Park. News from twenty-seven clubs around the US included numerous mentions of men in the forces. The mailbag was similarly biased towards the services. Lieutenant B.L. Elliot (Canadian Army Overseas) wrote: 'The army HDs are good, no doubt about it – they have proven their worth beside the other makes and made themselves popular with men who never rode bikes in civilian life. And that means a lot, for many of them will ride in peacetime now they have developed a liking for it in the army. But I long for civilian colors on the HDs again.' (GS)

The springer forks were replaced by hydraulic telescopic units in 1949 and the Big Twin was renamed the Hydra-Glide. The telescopic front end negated the need for the hydraulic damper but the remainder of the styling changes introduced for 1947 stayed current; tombstone tail-lights and similar are all to be found on early Panheads. In many ways the Hydra-Glide can be considered the crossover between the vintage-style Harleys and more modern machines. Whereas the springer forks looked vintage because of their exposed and spindly springs, the Hydra-Glide was much more modern in appearance with its larger diameter telescopic fork legs and a cast headlamp nacelle. In accordance with customer preference the sprung solo and buddy seats continued to be used in place of rear suspension, but Harley's engineers were working on this part of the motorcycle as the next major upgrade.

There were numerous smaller upgrades to the Hydra-Glide. In 1952 a customer-specified option of a foot gearshift was made available. Panheads equipped with this mechanism were designated FLF while the traditional handshift-fitted machine remained the FL. The basic E and F models were discontinued in 1952 and the smaller capacity EL, ELF and ES in 1953. From then on Panheads were available only as 74cid machines.

Changing Times

In addition to the introduction of the Panhead motor something else happened in 1948 that would propel the Harley-Davidson and its bastard offspring, the chopper, far beyond California's freeways. In March 1948 the first chapter of the Hell's Angels was founded in 'Berdoo' (San Bernardino, California). By 1954 the club was becoming established in 'Frisco' (San Francisco). It is recorded that in order to start another chapter a rider known as Rocky travelled north on a classic custom bike of the era. It was described as having tall 'ape-hanger' bars and chromed XA springer forks. (The latter components were the forks from the experimental Second World War Harley-Davidson and were 4 inches longer than stock springers. The cast VL springers from pre-war Big Twin flatheads were also desirable for early choppers because of their extra length.)

The origins of the chopper are inextricably linked with the period of American motorcycling that straddled the Second World War. Following the defeat of Japan US servicemen started coming home and many of them were looking for ways to spend their mustering-out pay and let off steam after a few years in uniform. A motorcycle was the perfect option. The war had a distinct influence on motorcycling in other ways too. Some say it led to the superstition that green Harleys are unlucky. Despatch riders were often considered a target by the enemy because they were likely to be carrying important information; the men also had to contend with dangerous journeys, land mines and wires strung across roads in forward areas to decapitate them.

For some of the war survivors who came home and started riding motorcycles again it was back to normal and back to AMA-sanctioned events. For others the transition was not so straightforward: motorcycle club uniforms and rally games did not hold the same appeal for restless combat veterans and those who had buried their comrades in Europe and the Pacific islands. James Jones, the author of

From Here to Eternity, summed it up: 'About the last thing to go was the sense of esprit. That was the hardest thing to let go of, because there was nothing in civilian life that could replace it. The love and understanding of men for men in dangerous times and places and situations. Just as there was nothing in civilian life that could replace the heavy, turgid, day-to-day excitement of danger. Families and other civilian types would never understand that sense of esprit any more than they would understand the excitement of the danger.' Some men found what they were looking for in the saddle of a big motorcycle, with equally restless buddies and the endless blacktop (road) – for better or worse the world had changed.

The first postwar Daytona 200 was run in 1947, the same year as the AMA rally, races and Gypsy Tour in Hollister, California. This latter, hitherto unremarkable event was about to become indelibly inked into the history books. Depending on which account you believe, the goings-on at Hollister over 4 July weekend were anything from a full-scale riot to little more than general rowdiness and beer drinking. The *San Francisco Chronicle* of Monday 7 July described it as 'The 40 hours that shook Hollister'.

The lines between fact and fiction have been blurred by time, and the fact that *Life* magazine, and subsequently movie-maker Stanley Kramer, picked up on the incident; otherwise it would probably have faded into obscurity as the newsprint yellowed. The beer drinking, spinning donuts, racing in the street and a few arrests for drunkenness would have simply been put down to 'the boys having too much fun'. Instead the result was the 1953 Columbia Pictures film *The Wild One*. It starred Marlon Brando and Lee Marvin and, regardless of the truth of its interpretation of the facts, it was pivotal in a number of respects. It set the style for future motorcyclists in terms of clothing and bikes. Brando, as the now legendary Johnny, wore a peaked cap and highway patrol jacket, while Marvin as his rival was every inch the up-and-coming outlaw biker in his sleeveless jacket, scruffy beard, cap comforter and goggles. Brando's Johnny fronted the Black Rebels MC and rode a Triumph twin, while Marvin did the same for the Beetles MC from the saddle of a chopped hog. Apart from inspiring hundreds of youngsters to copy the riders' styles of both clothes and motorcycles, the film, on a wider scale, incurred the wrath of an America edging its way towards the paranoia of McCarthyism. The country was becoming concerned about destabilisation and to some the film appeared to promote subversion and anti-social behaviour. It implied that motorcyclists were no-good hoodlums intent only on disrupting American life. This suggestion had already been made after the actual Hollister incident and the American Motorcyclist Association was keen to distance itself from the event, declaring that while 99 per cent of all motorcyclists were upstanding citizens 1 per cent were not. The 1 per cent label was to stick and was later adopted by the 'outlaw' clubs.

Bobbers and Choppers

The new British bikes were seen as competition for the two remaining American domestic manufacturers but were also a source of parts to use in building a chopper. H.R. Kaye describes an early 74 cubic inch chopper in *A Place in Hell*, which covers 'the early days' (although the period described is imprecisely dated): 'It was a

Bobbers like this one were the forerunners of choppers. They were often modified older bikes with tuned engines and were styled to resemble race bikes. This 45 uses RL-type forks from the '30s, cut down military-specification mudguards and a 45 cubic inch flathead engine with the later type alloy cylinder heads. (GS)

Model	Flathead Bobber	Power	23.5hp
Year	*c.* 1947	Carburettor	Linkert
Engine type	Flathead V-twin	Top speed	70mph
Displacement	45 cubic inches (739cc)	Frame	rigid, steel cradle
Bore and stroke	2.75×3.8 inches (70×97mm)	Forks	springers

masterpiece! The front fender had been removed and a Triumph front end installed. The rear fender was bobbed and chromed. It had dual headlights, ape-hangers, a custom tank and small leather saddle that had been pirated from an English racing machine. It had been painted black and polished to a blinding sheen. The engine was clean and neat as a pin.' The chopper in question was presumably a Knucklehead, 74 cubic inch variants of which were made in 1941 and 1946–47 or a 1948 Panhead, as these were the only years of 74 cubic inch Harleys made with springer forks. Had it already been fitted with telescopic forks there would have been little point in changing the front ends. Kaye called it Mariah, after the wind.

Custom parts were few and far between but the earliest styles had been established, having appeared in 'bobbers' (cut-down Harleys) and race bikes of the '40s and '50s. These early modified bikes coined the terminology and helped define certain parts, such as 'Fatbob' tanks – a bobber was a cut-down Harley but a Fatbob was a cut-down Harley that retained the stock two-piece tank the motor company used from 1936 onwards. Frame mods began after the Second World War and ape-hanger handlebars were made from crash-bars. Later, other 'custom' parts came from the K model – the solo seat for example – and the Sportster, which was introduced as the XL in 1957. The Sportster tank became a perennial favourite. The chopper's rear fender was still a front fender cut down; a front one was used because it had no hinge but followed the correct radius for the diameter of the wheel. Another trick was to use the more minimal fenders off a British bike – especially the ribbed ones – which made the Big Twins look more sleek.

One of the few companies making what can be termed custom parts was started by Lucile and Earl Flanders. Earl was a regular motorcycle competition rider who started making custom handlebars for other competitors after the war. He bent the tubes to suit his customer's requirements and manufactured them to specific widths – they became known as Flanders bars. Flanders risers also still bear his name; sometimes known as dog bones because of their shape, they are extension bars to lift the handlebars above the stock handlebar clamp.

Stroker motors became popular when mechanics started discovering that through mixing and matching Harley engine components it was possible to increase the capacity of a V-twin. One way to achieve this was to use the crank-pin, flywheels and con-rods out of the VL flathead engine and incorporate them into the later engines. The VL had a longer stroke than the overhead-valve engines and when used with the standard bore pistons increased the displacement without having to resort to expensive machining. The nickname of 'stroker' is self-explanatory: the engine's capacity was raised by increasing the stroke.

Riding on a Boom

Boom years followed the introduction of the Panhead engine and in 1948 the company sold 31,163 bikes. But the boom was not to last. Imports from Europe flooded the US market. Indian could not compete and closed in 1953. Harley-Davidson preferred to tackle the competition head on and introduced motorcycles designed to do exactly that. The K model, introduced in 1952, was a curious mixture of old and new: the last 45 cubic inch WL-series flathead had been made in 1951 but a new design of flathead engine was fitted to the new motorcycle.

The K was a unit construction 45 cubic inch (750cc) flathead V-twin-engined bike with a foot change/hand clutch transmission aimed at competing with the imported British motorcycles. It was assembled around a swing-arm frame fitted with telescopic forks. The side-valve engine was vastly slower than the imports and the KK model was introduced in response to criticisms of the speed of the K. The K's main drawback was its performance, so in 1954 the KH, a developed version, was introduced. It used a K model engine with a lengthened stroke which meant its displacement went up to 53 cubic inches (883cc). It also had new flywheels, cylinder barrels, an improved clutch and was generally a better motorcycle . It could compete with the British imports on more even terms. The KH remained in production until 1956 when it was replaced by the models designated XL, the first of the motorcycles referred to as Sportsters. The K and KH models resembled their foreign competitors in styling in that they had a swinging-arm rear suspension assembly, telescopic forks, foot gearshift and neat compact lines.

Side-valve engines were considered decidedly old fashioned by the late '50s and were quickly being superseded by overhead-valve engines. However, this did not stop the dominance of the side-valve on dirt tracks the length and breadth of America. Harley-Davidson built the KR for racing and its engine included important differences from the K model. The valve arrangement had changed, camshafts with different profiles were used and the engine relied on ball- rather than roller-bearings. The KR, KRTT, KRM and KHR remained in production until 1968.

For now, though, the Panhead-powered Harleys were kings of the road.

This snapshot from someone's family album illustrates the postwar use of many ex-military motorcycles. It is a WLC converted into a sidecar outfit and civilianised to provide family transport. The photograph was taken in a town in the north of England. Dealers such as Pride & Clarke of London sold large amounts of war surplus motorcycles and clothing. (AC)

The pits at Daytona Beach, prior to the 200 mile race of 1954. No. 96 is a race-prepared WL Harley typical of the era. Note the tank pad, pillion pad and bobbed mudguards. Also present are racers from the Bush Riders of Dekalb, Illinois. British bikes are also in evidence in this photo and the 1954 race was won by Bobby Hill on a BSA. The first nine places were taken by BSA and Triumph machines, although tenth and eleventh places went to Harley-mounted Don Hutchinson and Leon Applegate respectively. (AC)

Carroll Resweber, seen here on a race-prepared 45 – note the Flanders-type risers and dirt track tyres – was from Port Arthur, Texas. Initially he rode a Knucklehead stroked to 80cid through the use of U model flywheels. In 1952 he started racing and, on a bike built by Ralph Berndt with a KR engine, was National Champion in 1958, 1959, 1960 and 1961. He retired after a bad crash at the Lincoln half-mile while he was leading the 1962 championship. (AC)

Opposite: The '50s saw a return to many of the traditions of pre-war motorcycling, including gypsy tours and motorcycle club uniforms. Peaked caps, leather flying helmets and club jerseys were worn by both male and female riders. Windshields were a popular addition to Hydra-Glides and children can be seen in both sidecars in this photograph, confirming that many riders saw motorcycling as a family pastime. It is interesting to note that one sidecar has a luggage rack fitted in the manner of a car roof-rack. (HD)

The Hydra-Glide was the first Harley-Davidson Big Twin to feature hydraulic telescopic forks. The model name, Hydra-Glide, originates from this feature. It replaced the springer-forked Panhead in Harley-Davidson's range and was introduced in 1949. The Hydra-Glide did not feature rear suspension but relied on the sprung saddle to ensure the rider's comfort over long journeys. The panniers and an optional windshield helped make the Hydra-Glide suitable for long-distance riding. The chrome trims either side of the rear light are period accessories. (HD)

During the mid-'50s Harley-Davidson offered the Panhead-powered FL Hydra-Glide models with a choice of the traditional hand shift/foot clutch arrangement or the more modern hand clutch/foot change one. The FLF was the foot clutch variant and is seen here about to be filled up with Mobilgas. (AC)

The load-carrying ability of the Servicar endeared it to numerous business users, including garage proprietors who despatched their mechanics to breakdowns with tools and spares stored in the cargo body. Garages also used to collect customers' cars for servicing with a Servicar and returned to the garage towing the Servicar with a special bumper attachment. This one is being used to spray water in an American suburb. (NMM)

The Servicar found favour with numerous American police departments for a variety of duties, including emptying parking meters and dispensing parking tickets. This one, from the late '40s, is equipped with a radiator. It has an aerial fitted to the side of the load box and was used for monitoring parking meters. To the rider's right on the windshield is a pole with a fitting for a coloured chalk in the end. The rider rode past parked cars and marked the windshields with the chalk. After a suitable interval he would return and would know that any with the coloured mark had exceeded the allotted period for parking. (NMM)

6

Panhead to Shovelhead
1955–1968

Details of the Harley range were redesigned in 1955 and included the change to the three-light dash, which featured an extra warning light over the two of earlier models. The three new lights were circular and located in different positions from the two rectangular ones used from 1947 to 1955. The top-of-the-range Big Twin for 1955 was the FLH; it had a stronger bottom end and higher compression. It was the FLH that inspired the term 'dresser', because owners of the Big Twins used to accessorise their machines with saddlebags and windshields. Initially these were made from leather and canvas but as times moved on they were manufactured from glassfibre and plastic. The big bikes, which looked even bigger with the accessories, came to be referred to as 'dressed'. Harley-Davidson had always marketed a line of official accessories and began to offer such equipment off the showroom floor.

Duo-Glide and Electra-Glide

The rigid frame of the Hydra-Glide was finally upgraded to swing-arm rear suspension in the Duo-Glide in 1958. The name Duo-Glide was based on the fact that the new models had a 'Glide' at both ends and Harley trumpeted this feature by renaming the Big Twin models, although there were still FL an FLH motorcycles too. The Big Twin was renamed again when the electric start appeared in 1965 and became the Electra-Glide (the hyphen in the name was later dropped). In effect the Electra-Glide was a Duo-Glide with electric start.

Alongside these improvements and modifications to the frame and forks of the big-twin-powered motorcycles there were numerous detail developments to the engine. In fact, in all there were six different Panhead engines. The first had been made between 1948 and 1953 in both 61 and 74 cubic inch capacities. The second type, with a different pinion shaft, was manufactured only in 1954. The bearings on the engine sprocket shaft were altered for the third type, which appeared in 1955, when a spring-loaded shock-absorbing sprocket was incorporated and the lubrication system was change slightly. The fourth change came in 1958 when the pinion shaft was altered to accept larger main bearings and this was how the motor stayed until 1963. In that year, however, the oil feed to the cylinder heads was taken through an external oil line to create the fifth version. The final changes to the Panhead affected the engine's cases and covers, and meant it could now take an electric starter.

The Duo-Glide was superseded by the Hydra-Glide with the addition of rear suspension in 1958. The bike was still powered by the proven Panhead engine (1948–65). The new tank badge, seen here, was introduced in 1959 and used again in 1960. The two-into-one exhaust was standard, while HD offered both hand- and foot-shift gearchange models. (GS)

Model	FLH Duo-Glide	Power	52hp
Year	1959	Carburettor	Schebler
Engine type	OHV V-twin Panhead	Top speed	100mph
Displacement	74 cubic inches (1208cc)	Frame	swing-arm, steel cradle
Bore and stroke	3.44×3.97 inches (87×101mm)	Forks	telescopic

The Advent of the Sportster

Harley-Davidson upgraded the KH model to an overhead-valve configuration in 1957 and redesignated it the XL; it became known as the Sportster. The first XL Sportster engine displaced 53 cubic inches (883cc), although by the early '70s there was a 61cid (1000cc) model available in a range including the XL, XLCH, XLT, XLX which stayed in production until the introduction of the Evolution-engined

Al Gunter (no. 54) on a KH model, 1955. Although Gunter was a skilled racer he never won at Daytona. He did, however, finish in the top ten five times and was the fastest qualifier in 1957. He was a Californian from the Los Angeles area and raced regularly at the famous Ascot track where he won the 8 mile National Dirt Track championship race eight times. (DM)

Sportsters in 1986. Unlike the Big Twin Harleys, Sportsters featured unit construction, meaning that the engine and gearbox were both part of one casting rather than two separate items. The early Sportsters were noted for being fast yet fragile, although these characteristics were modified as the years passed and it got stronger.

The Sportster name has endured until the present and the development of this model has paralleled that of the Big Twins. The first XLH came in 1958 with a higher compression ratio than the XL. It was followed by the XLCH. The electrical system was upgraded to 12 volts in 1965 in line with the FL models and an electric start XL was made available in 1967.

Servicars

The three-wheeler Servicar was upgraded with the introduction of an electric start in 1964 when its model designation was changed from G to GE. This meant that the humble working Servicar was actually the first Harley-Davidson to come equipped with an electric starter – the mighty Electra-Glide did not appear until 1965.

The differences between pre- and post-1964 Servicars are easy to spot as the later machines have a large alternator mounted on the frame downtube. The starter itself is mounted on top of the transmission and drives the outer clutch hub to start the engine. The large unit was deemed necessary to charge the battery sufficiently to ensure there was enough power for starting.

Some further changes to the Servicar were made in conjunction with those made to the solos and other alterations to the three-wheeler came independently. Examples of the latter include the shift from spoked wheels to pressed-steel ones at the rear, and from steel load boxes to moulded glassfibre ones. Production ran until 1973.

The Chopper Comes of Age

It was around this time that the chopper became an up-and-coming fashion; some Harley riders accessorised their bikes to dress them up so others, possibly as a reaction, effectively undressed them by chopping everything off. The bikes treated in this way bore a strong resemblance to the earlier race-style bobbers, at least for a while, but later developed fashions all their own, including over-length forks, small tanks taken from scooters and mopeds, jockey-shift gearchanges and numerous other details. Choppers are mentioned here because these unofficial styles became so important to Harley riders around the US that in the later Shovelhead era, Harley-Davidson started offering mildly custom models in dealers' showrooms and invented the concept of the 'factory custom'.

The ape-hangered chopper evolved from the race-influenced bobber in an imprecise way. It wasn't that the clock stopped on one style then started for another. Styles simply metamorphosed from one to another in the manner of a kaleidoscope – and given the counter-culture, the summer of love and the psychedelic times that are said to characterise the '60s, that seems to be an appropriate analogy.

George Wethern documented the early '60s in *Wayward Angel* (1979): 'In 1960, there were relatively few custom shops where dollars could be swapped for a sleek,

The chopper as a form of motorcycle was indirectly promoted right around the world in 1969 with the release of the film *Easy Rider*. This early chopper was built in England. It uses a Harley Davidson 45 side-valve engine, the only Harley widely available in Europe at that time because of the plentiful supply of ex-military WLA and WLC machines, along with the Harley 45 transmission, frame and rear wheel, which has been modified. Other parts have been made, modified or bought including the long custom springer forks and the fuel tank from a British bike. The handlebars, seat, cissybar and mudguards are custom parts. (BSH)

chrome stallion. Grooming one yourself was the surest way to get a worthy mount.' He went on to describe the process: 'In addition to about $3,000, you needed mechanical know-how and energy to break down and refine a seventy-four-cubic-inch Harley-Davidson that rolled from the factory with doughnut tyres, a bulbous gas tank, heavy fenders and vanity-size mirrors and an uninspiring paintjob. We called them garbage wagons, but the 700lb Harley stockers rolled like two-wheeled Cadillacs.' It was clear that a stock Harley was regarded only as the raw material from which a chopper would emerge: 'Behind the piggish profile was amazing power waiting to be freed with welding torches, wrenches and screwdrivers. With the cycle stripped to the bare frame, the engine was torn down, bored out to eighty cubic inches, pumped up in horsepower. A bicycle-sized twenty-one inch front wheel was fitted to extended front forks that raked back the cut down frame, the effect multiplied by riser handlebars with silver dollar-sized mirrors. The fenders were thrown away or bobbed to the legal minimum. The cushy banana seat was thrown away and replaced with a lean saddle, the gas tank exchanged for a stinger with a

The chopper fad started in California and spread rapidly. This Knucklehead is typical of '50s choppers and is built from a mixture of Harley-Davidson parts. It uses chromed VL springer forks, a Sportster fuel tank, a K-model solo seat, upswept fishtail pipes and a Knucklehead engine. Other non-standard parts include a Bates headlamp and a flat rear fender.

twelve coat finish of lacquer. Finally, chrome pipes snorting, the beast stood ready to buck with a chomp of metal gears.' The finished bike was acknowledged as being 200lb lighter and therefore faster because of both the improved power to weight ratio and the tuned engine.

California Hell's Angel, Freewheeling Frank, writing of the same era in 1967, defined a chopper in much the same vein and noted its origins as the particular choice of the 1 per cent identified by the AMA. He wrote: 'A chopper means a Harley-Davidson motorcycle that has been stripped of extra accessories, including the fenders and tanks, which leaves only the frame and engine. These are then replaced with small fenders and one tank – along with straight pipes as the main changes. This leaves the motorcycle looking like a lean and furious monster. It's our creation, of our breed of horse. We love them.' Hunter S. Thompson in his seminal book about the California Hell's Angels of the mid-'60s wrote of the chopper of the time: 'It is a beautiful, graceful machine and so nearly perfect mechanically'. So it was.

The '60s were the era of LSD and free love, of beautiful people and hippies, of the Vietnam War (the US Marine Corps deployed in South Vietnam in 1965 as the USA assumed a full combat role in South-East Asia) and the protests against it. The late

The Electra-Glide was the final incarnation of the Panhead. It was a Duo-Glide with an electric starter introduced in 1965. The Shovelhead-powered Electra-Glide, seen here, appeared in 1966 and was Harley-Davidson's first Big Twin to be equipped with an electric starter. However, he first electric start Harley was the 1964 Servicar three-wheeler. (GS)

Model	FLH Electra-Glide	Power	54hp
Year	1966	Carburettor	Linkert
Type	OHV V-twin Shovelhead	Top speed	100mph
Displacement	74 cubic inches (1208cc)	Frame	swing-arm, steel cradle
Bore and stroke	3.44×3.97 inches (87×101mm)	Forks	telescopic

'60s saw America bitterly divided over the issues surrounding the Vietnam War. The belief that the Hell's Angels were the defenders of counter-culture and the flower people's guardians had been exposed as a myth in 1965: the Oakland Hell's Angels interrupted an anti-war protest march from radical Berkeley towards the Army Depot in Oakland. The truth was that in the main bikers tended to be blue collar in upbringing and outlook while the radical liberals were middle class.

The Birth of the Shovelhead

From 1948 to 1965 the Panhead was king and its distinctive top-end clatter was a familiar and beloved sound. The Panhead engine was superseded by the Shovelhead in 1966. Once again Harley engineers had come up with a development that was essentially a new top end fitted to an existing bottom end. The new engine became known as the Shovelhead because the rocker covers bear a similarity to the back of an upturned shovel. It may seem contrived but as a nickname it is now universal.

Most of the new models had designations that started FL – the FLB, FLHB and so on. The B suffix denoted electric start and was used until 1969, but was dropped for 1970, presumably because the back-up kick starter had been discontinued. The new engine featured the same bore and stroke as all 74 cubic inch Big Twins back as far as 1941, but not all the parts of these various powerplants were interchangeable. Some other components, such as the dash panel and lights, were also redesigned in 1966, although the tank-mounted speedo and ignition switch remained. The tombstone tail-light disappeared in favour of a more rectangular unit.

By the mid-'60s Harley-Davidson's share of the US domestic motorcycle market had contracted considerably and only 3 per cent of its production was being exported. It became clear that Harley – the last American motorcycle manufacturer – would go the way of Indian unless it received substantial investment. In 1969 Harley-Davidson was bought by American Machine and Foundry, a huge conglomerate that owned a variety of leisure and industrial companies. AMF took control of Harley-Davidson on 7 January 1969. It was not an entirely happy marriage and led to a strike over job losses, quality control problems and all the other symptoms of dissatisfied industry.

As if to demonstrate that Harley-Davidson was unbeaten despite the takeover, Cal Rayborn rode a KR model to victory in the Daytona 200 race. It was Harley's last victory in the famous Florida race. On the street the 'Ironhead' Sportster engine and the Shovelhead-powered Harley-Davidson road-going bikes persisted through the '70s and the years of AMF ownership.

The staff of *Motorcycling* – a weekly British motorcycle magazine – tested this 1950 74cid model, a Hydra-Glide, and reported on it in their edition of 8 December 1955. The bike was loaned to the magazine by Technical Sergeant E.R. Berry of the USAF who was stationed at the Burtonwood airbase in Lancashire. The owner had upgraded the Panhead to 1955 specification by fitting a foot gearshift and hand clutch. Despite the fact that the British and American motorcycles differed considerably in the '50s, the magazine was favourably impressed by the Hydra-Glide. (AC)

The Hydra-Glide became the Duo-Glide in 1958 but as late as 1957 Harley-Davidson was still promoting improvements to the rigid-framed model. The company had redesigned the bottom end of the Panhead engine in 1955. The new engine looked similar to its predecessor but featured stronger main bearings and slightly redesigned crankcases. (GS)

Adventure ahead

74 OHV HARLEY-DAVIDSON
'57 HYDRA-GLIDES

MODEL FL

FIRST CHOICE IN AMERICA . . . THE SUPERLINER FL

You're way ahead with a Hydra-Glide® . . . on the expressways and byways of America. Way ahead for sheer luxury . . . way ahead for thrilling power . . . way ahead for dependability. Here is motorcycling enjoyment . . . plus! Sure, steady power coupled with a smooth, gliding ride. Wherever you find motorcyclists . . . you'll find Hydra-Glides® outnumbering all others by a wide margin. It's *first* in America . . . and the finest in the world!

MODEL FLH

AHEAD . . . WAY AHEAD WITH THE SUPER-POWERED FLH

For the rider who wants to be a leader among leaders . . . it's the power-packed FLH with that extra thrust! Up to sixty horsepower is compactly contained in this sensational Hydra-Glide® . . . poised and ready to deliver a whole new world of thrilling experiences at the flick of a wrist. You'll tingle at the unbelievable, surging "take-off" of this custom-built model. Words can't begin to describe the riding sensations of the Hydra-Glide® FLH. Your first ride will tell you . . . you'll be way ahead with an FLH in '57.

HARLEY-DAVIDSON MOTOR CO.
Milwaukee 1, Wisconsin, U. S. A.

F E A T U R E S

FLH FEATURES

1. *How the FLH gets its GO. Cylinder head showing super-polished intake ports.*

2. *Attractive shield emblem on the oil tank sets you apart as the owner of a custom-built FLH Model.*

3. *New FLH aluminum alloy piston, with new, power-retaining narrow compression rings. Compression ratio increased to 8 to 1.*

4. *FLH, high-lift "Victory" cam results in greater horsepower and acceleration.*

FOR ALL HYDRA-GLIDES

5. *Smooth operating, multiple dry disc clutch. Built for rugged use—high torque capacity, dependable.*

6. *Stop! Safe, sure internal expanding brakes, front and rear. Fully enclosed and waterproof.*

7. *The famous Hydra-Glide® fork produces the perfect ride. Hydraulically-controlled spring fork does the work.*

8. *New, improved push rods permit greater amount of rod adjustment and result in easier removal of push rods in service work.*

NEW, MORE DURABLE H-D 100 FINISHES

New formula enamel stays better looking . . . longer. Needs no waxing. Resists scratches and dents. Luxurious color selection: Skyline Blue, Birch White, Pepper Red, Black, Metallic Midnight Blue (extra cost).

1958 Duo-Glide. The Duo-Glide was the logical extension of the Hydra-Glide, an FL with 'Glides' at both ends. It was introduced in 1958 in both FL and FLH forms. The Panhead engine supplied the get up and go. The earlier E and F models with lower compression had been dropped and so the new bottom end was suitable for the more powerful FLH model. The FLF was a footshift/hand clutch variant. It is acknowledged that Harley-Davidson kept both the FLF and the FLH in production in order to satisfy all its customers. (GS)

Above and opposite: The Duo-Glide for 1960 was an opulent touring motorcycle for which a dazzling array of accessories was available, including fibreglass rear panniers, tinted screens, chromed mudguard bars, whitewall tyres, exhaust covers, dual seat, luggage carriers and optional colours, including 'Hi-Fi' red and white. Chrome covers on the shock absorbers, trumpet horns and suchlike were all typical of the era and led to the bikes being referred to as 'dressers' or more disparagingly 'garbage wagons'. The FLH designation had been new for 1955: the H indicated polished ports and Victory camshafts, i.e. H for 'hopped up' or 'hot'. (GS)

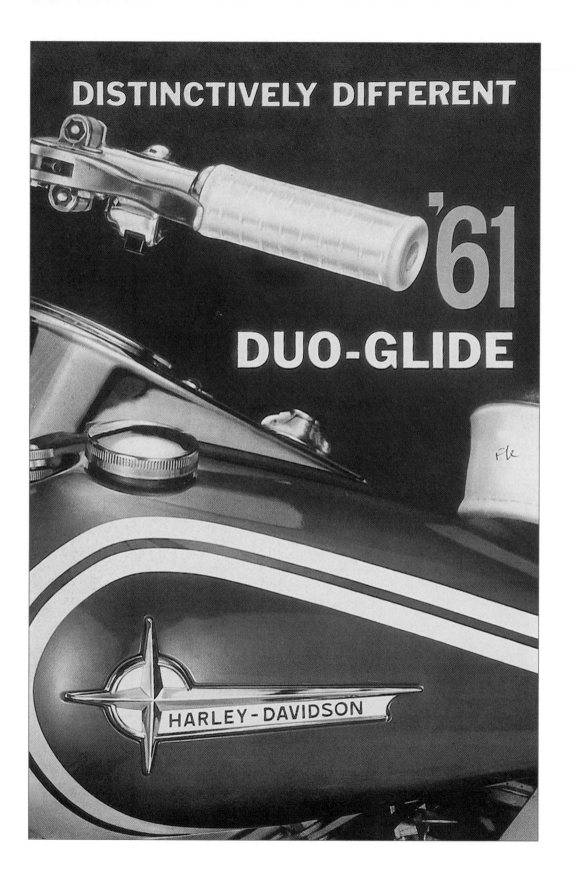

The 1961 Duo-Glide range brochure promoted the new year's models and highlighted the detail and option upgrades. (GS)

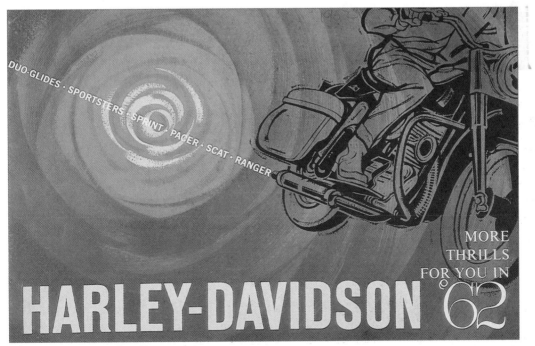

The 1962 range brochure also outlined new extras and options; the big news was to come with the addition of the electric starter in 1965. (GS)

Many US police departments bought Harley-Davidsons for traffic duties. This was important business for the company which went as far as to produce special police motorcycle brochures, including this Duo-Glide one. Many US police departments still use Harley-Davidsons and over the years police Harley-Davidsons have appeared in films such as *Electraglide in Blue* and *JFK*. The bikes in use at the time the latter film was set would have been Duo-Glides. (GS)

By 1960 the three-wheeler Servicar was the only Harley-Davidson still using the 22bhp 45cid side-valve engine as its powerplant. The basic concept of the Servicar as a utility machine remained unchanged, although details had been upgraded – fibreglass load boxes, pressed-steel rear wheels and telescopic forks were all fitted. In the final years of Servicar production even an electric start (from 1964) and a disc brake (from 1972) were fitted. The machine's 42-year production run ended in 1973. (GS)

The US scooter market flourished during the '50s and Harley-Davidson introduced its version in 1959. Scooters were easy to ride and offered cheap transport for youngsters. The Topper featured a centrifugal clutch, a two-stroke engine, a belt-drive system that offered automatic gearing and 12-inch diameter wheels. The 165cc Topper did not have the curvaceous lines of the Italian Lambretta and Vespa designs and it was not the sales success it might have been. Toppers were dropped from Harley-Davidson's line in 1965 but were still going strong in 1961, as this Topper brochure suggests. A Topper starred briefly in the TV series *77 Sunset Strip*. (GS)

Harley-Davidson wanted to sell entry-level bikes in the USA and had marketed the 125cc two-stroke Hummer. The company came to the conclusion that it could not build small bikes cheaply enough in the US so bought a controlling interest in the Italian firm Aermacchi. One of the Aermacchi's models was a four-stroke 250cc (15cid) single. Its cylinder projected forwards horizontally and the machine had a four-speed transmission, hand clutch and foot shift, and swinging-arm rear suspension. The first Aermacchi for the US market was given the factory code of C, named the Sprint and imported for the 1961 sales season. (GS)

Action during the 1956 Daytona 200 at the South Turn. The race used the Atlantic coast beach and a parallel road as the main straights with turns linking the two to comprise a course of just over 4 miles. Johnny Gibson won the race aboard a Harley and finished ahead of four BSAs which were followed by another five Harleys. (AC)

A photograph that illustrates how close dirt-track racing gets: Al Gunter (no. 3) on a Harley and George Everett (no. 84) on a British bike tangle on a turn during a race at California's Gardena Stadium in 1956. (DM)

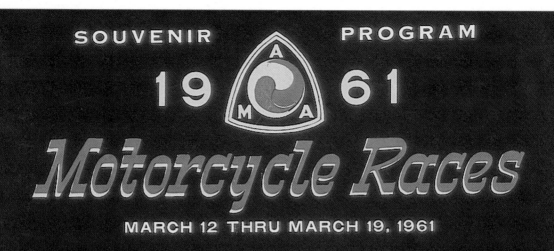

The cover of the programme for the 1961 Daytona 200 motorcycle race features the AMA's logo prominently. The 1961 running of the event was the first to use the new purpose-built speedway track. The AMA had reservations about motorcycles racing on the 33-degree banked turns so a 2 mile course in the infield was used. The event was won by 22-year-old Roger Reiman on a Harley-Davidson KR 750. He covered the 200 mile distance in 2 hours, 53 minutes, 17.15 seconds, averaging 69.25mph. He had held the lead from the second lap onwards. (GS)

Left to right: dirt-track race promoter J.C. Agajanian with the father and son team of Leonard Andres and Brad Andres after Brad won an event aboard his KR. (DM)

Joe Leonard (no. 98) on a KR model. Leonard
was an accomplished rider who had a successful
career racing Harleys. He won the Daytona 200
in 1957 and 1958 as well as twenty-five other
AMA National Championship races. He was the
AMA Grand National Champion in 1954, 1956
and 1957. He went on to race Indy cars. (DM)

Left to right: trophy girl Ginger Wilde, racer
Joe Leonard and promoter J.C. Agajanian after
a Leonard win during 1959 at De Anza,
California. Note that the bike has a front drum
brake. (DM)

The KH evolved into the XL Sportster of 1957 which soon gained its own identity. By 1958 the Sportster brochure was able to point out that the machine's horsepower had been increased through bigger ports and valves. There were to be numerous versions of the Sportster over the next forty-plus years. (GS)

In 1957 the XL Sportster made its debut. It was a 55cid overhead-valve V-twin-engined motorcycle with an integral four-speed transmission. It featured an oil bath primary chain drive and sealed dry clutch. The bike was based around a swing-arm frame and telescopic forks. It was soon followed by the XLCH which was a more basic motorcycle that debuted in 1958 and the XLH of 1960. (HD)

Harley-Davidson built the KR for racing. It comprised a flathead V-twin engine in a rigid frame. The factory also built the KRTT in a swinging-arm frame for TT events and a lesser known model, the KRM, for desert racing. Joe Leonard is seen here at the 1959 Ascot TT on a KRTT. It features rear suspension and shock absorbers, K brakes front and rear, and a damped rather than sprung solo seat. (DM)

Joe Leonard (no. 98) on a Sportster. The Sportster was initially an overhead-valve version of the K model. The Sportster displaced 53 cubic inches (883cc) and in stock form produced 32bhp at 4200rpm. The unit construction XL had a four-speed transmission and was capable of 90mph. The bike, with drum brakes, telescopic forks and a swinging-arm rear suspension, was comparable with the imported British bikes with which it had to compete for sales. (DM)

Troy Lee (no. 16) on a dirt-track-prepared KR during the late '50s. The motorcycle has a less aggressive front tyre than was frequently used, which Lee must have considered offered better performance at this particular track. The large air-filter was designed to maximise the engine's breathing while preventing dust ingress. (DM)

Californian Johnny Gibson (no. 5), seen here on a KR, raced at Daytona in 1951 and 1953 on British bikes, a BSA and a Norton respectively, but switched to Harleys for 1955. In that year he finished third but a year later won the race which was then nicknamed the 'Handlebar Derby' because of its close racing. Gibson raced at Daytona again in 1958, 1959 and 1960 but did not repeat his victory. (DM)

XLCH Sportsters photographed at De Anza in 1958. The XLCH was new for this year and had been introduced in response to demands from the West Coast for a stripped down Sportster suitable for scrambling and other forms of competition. The competition version seen here had the rear fender bobbed just behind the strut and the front fender removed. The Sportster in this form was a brutal-looking and functional motorcycle. (DM)

A 1960 Sportster being ridden in England. Great Britain had only one franchised Harley-Davidson dealer for many years, namely Fred Warr's in London. This number gradually increased but it was not until the advent of the Evolution range of Harleys in the '80s that dealers (and customers) became plentiful. (AC)

The Electra-Glide was introduced in 1965. It was essentially a Duo-Glide with the addition of an electric starter as its name suggested. Power for the new model came from the proven Panhead engine although this was replaced by the new 'Shovelhead' a year later and subsequently by the Evolution and Twin Cam engines. (HD)

Model	FLH Electra-Glide	Power	60hp
Year	1965	Carburettor	Linkert
Engine type	OHV V-twin Panhead	Top speed	100mph
Displacement	74 cubic inches (1208cc)	Frame	swing-arm, steel cradle
Bore and stroke	3.44×3.97 inches (87×101mm)	Forks	telescopic

In 1965 *Cycle World* magazine tested an XLH Sportster. It achieved 0–60mph in 7.4 seconds and in the standing quarter mile it reached 84mph and an elapsed time of 15.5 seconds. The bike in question had 18 inch diameter wheels back and front, a wheelbase of 57 inches, a seat height of 30.5 inches and a 3.75 gallon fuel tank. (HD)

The 1966 XLH Sportster was one of the kick-start 53cid (883cc) motorcycles made between 1957 and 1967. Electric start was not available until 1967 and disc brakes were not fitted until 1973. The '60s XLH was considered a sports-tourer by Harley-Davidson but it was outsold by the XLCH, seen here, because the latter looked better. Some said the CH indicated 'Competition Hot'. The XLCH featured the classic Sportster tank and was a more basic, brutal motorcycle. (HD)

George Roeder (no. 94) at the Sacramento Mile in 1966. Roeder, from Monroeville, Ohio, was a competitive rider on circuits and on the dirt tracks. He also rode one of two streamliners on the salt flats at Bonneville, Utah. The streamliner, built by James Mangham, was powered by a short-stroke 250cc Harley-Davidson Sprint engine and Roeder was clocked at 176.817mph in it in 1965. (DM)

Bart Markel, seen here in 1966, was never the most successful of Harley racers on surfaced race tracks but was one of the all-time greats of dirt-track racing. He won twenty-eight National Championship races and was AMA Grand National Champion in 1962, 1965 and 1966. Markel's highest placing at Daytona was achieved in 1961 when he finished fifth behind the Harley-Davidsons of winner Roger Reiman and George Roeder (third). Riders on British bikes placed second and fourth. (DM)

To take the National Championship in 1966, Bart Markel notched up a win at the Columbus dirt track then placed second at Elkhorn and Heidelberg. At the Ascot TT he finished tenth. He followed this with a seventh at the Greenwood, Iowa, road race, second at Lincoln, Illinois, and second at Springfield. Following this he won the Short Track National at Santa Fe, took second in the Peoria TT and second at the 8 mile National at Ascot. This fortunately secured him sufficient points to take the championship because engine problems dogged his ride in the Carlsbad, California, road race and the Sacramento Mile dirt track leading to sixteenth and fifth place finishes respectively. (DM)

Close racing! John Tibben (no. 60) on his rigid Aermacchi racer at the Long Beach indoor concrete short track during 1966 with Bob Bailey close behind. (DM)

120

Ron Ermels (no. 11) and Phil Hawk (no. 8) during the mid-'60s with Harley-Davidson KRs. By this time some of the riders were using after-market parts such as Ceriani forks and frames made from thin-wall chrome molybdenum steel to ensure the Harleys were competitive when faced with competition from British bikes. (DM)

Darrell Duval (no. 45) 'tucked in' on a KR at the Sacramento Mile during 1966. The configuration of the unit-construction flathead-powered motorcycle is clearly evident here, as are the telescopic forks and alloy wheels with fat dirt track tyres and no brakes. (DM)

Mert Lawwill at the Ascot TT in 1966. TT indicates Tourist Trophy although in American racing a TT event is considerably different from the European version, such as the famed Isle of Man races. The US-type TT is held on a dirt track but incorporates jumps and turns in both directions. Brakes and suspension were needed to cope with the courses and Harley-Davidson incorporated both features in its TT version of the KR model, known as the KRTT. Road-racing Harley-Davidsons used the KRTT frame and brakes; they were additionally equipped with fairings and larger capacity fuel tanks. (DM)

The Harley-Davidson KR was the racing version of the K model and was introduced in 1952. The dirt-track version of the KR – seen here with Mert Lawwill aboard at the Ascot Half-Mile in 1966 – had a rigid rear end with the wheel held in place in a subframe that bolted to the main frame at the end of the top tube and behind the gearbox. The KR had a long production run and was increasingly tuned during it. The first models produced approximately 38bhp and the last, manufactured in 1969, around 60bhp. (DM)

The fact that side-valve-engined motorcycles were still being raced competitively in the USA during the mid-'60s (as seen here with Mert Lawwill's KR in 1966) was largely down to slow changes in the motorcycle racing rules set by the AMA. (DM)

Bart Markel (no. 1), Mel Lacher (no. 37) and Chris Draayer (no. 77) at Tulare, California, in 1967. Draayer, a Mormon from Salt Lake City, Utah, was a newcomer to the Harley-Davidson team for 1966. He raced at Daytona in 1966 and 1967. Mel Lacher competed at Daytona in 1964, 1965 and 1966; he was the fastest qualifier in 1965, when the race was run in heavy rain, and so started in pole position. He went out after only four laps. (DM)

Bart Markel at Tulare. This 5 mile National win was Markel's second and last of the 1967 season. Tulare was known as a dimly lit dirt track with a rough surface – some riders preferred not to compete there. Markel rebuilt his engine between practice and the main event with assistance from other Harley riders Cal Rayborn, George Roeder and Roger Reiman. Despite this win, Markel did not take the championship. (DM)

Speaking of Bart Markel – three time Grand National Championship winner – in 1967, his wife Jo Ann said: 'This coming season, 1967, will be like all the others. The other guys, and I think especially Gary Nixon, will all be trying to take Number One away from Bart. It's a lot of pressure to have on you, but Bart doesn't talk about it.' Nixon and his Triumph did indeed win the no. 1 plate that year. (DM)

Fred Nix (no. 95) on a flathead Harley ahead of Gene Romero (no. 20) on a Triumph during a half-mile race at Oklahoma City, 1967. (DM)

In late 1967 Bart Markel, Mert Lawwill, Cal Rayborn and Chris Draayer went to Sedalia, Missouri, to enter a mile dirt-track race held in conjunction with the state fair. The track was rough and lacking in safety hay bales. During the race Draayer, seen here, was involved in an accident caused by Markel's engine seizing. Draayer hit the perimeter fence and was seriously injured, suffering a broken leg, internal injuries and the loss of one arm. Markel was sickened by the accident but Draayer accepted that it wasn't Markel's fault. (DM)

Mert Lawwill (no. 18) and Dan Haaby (no. 22) photographed on rigid-framed KR racers in 1967. The KRs were great bikes for dirt-track racing and because of this they had a production run that far outlasted the road-going K and KH models. The power extracted from the side-valve engines was increased as the years passed thanks to the ingenuity of the tuners and race mechanics. (DM)

Harley-Davidson team riders in 1967. From left to right: Bart Markel (no. 1), Mert Lawwill (no. 18), Mel Lacher (no. 37), Chris Draayer (no. 77) and Fred Nix (no. 95). That times were changing in the motorcycle industry for Harley-Davidson (and the British factories) is evidenced by the Suzuki advertising in this photograph which was indicative of the rising tide of imported Japanese motorcycles. (DM)

Fred Nix was new to the Harley-Davidson team for 1966 and won five National Championship events in the 1968 season. These results left him duelling with Gary Nixon (Triumph) for the championship. It was decided in the last event of the season when Nixon finished ahead of Nix at Ascot, ensuring Nixon retained the no. 1 plate. Nix was killed in a car accident during 1969. (DM)

For 1968 Bart Markel from Flint had the no. 4 plate. He is seen here in February of that year checking the rear axle of his Aermacchi HD Sprint-based CR short-track racer. Note that the rigid frame depends on a huge top tube for strength and to carry the engine, while a number of smaller diameter tubes provide a rigid rear-axle mount. (DM)

Acknowledgements

The author is indebted to the following for their assistance with photographs for this book: Harley-Davidson Motor Company, Imperial War Museum, National Motor Museum, John Bolt, BSH magazine, Garry Stuart and especially Dan Mahoney for all the dirt track pictures.

Picture Credits

AC   Author's Collection
BSH   *Back Street Heroes* magazine
DM   Dan Mahoney
GS   Garry Stuart
HD   Harley Davidson Motor Co.
JC   John Carroll
NMM   National Motor Museum

Bibliography

Jones, J., *World War II*, Leo Cooper, 1975
Kaye, H.R., *A Place in Hell*, Holloway House Publishing Co., 1968
Mauldin, Bill, *The Brass Ring*, W.W. Norton & Co. Inc, 1971
Reynolds, F., and McClure, M., *Freewheelin' Frank*, Grove Press Inc, 1967
Scalzo, J., *The Bart Markel Story*, Bond/Parkhurst Books, 1972
Thompson, H.S., *Hell's Angels*, Random House, 1966
Wethern, G., and Colnett, V., *A Wayward Angel*, Transworld Publishers, 1979